Values-Based Teaching Skills

Introduction & Implementation

BRIAN P. HALL
Santa Clara University

JANET KALVEN
The Grailville Conference Center, Loveland, Ohio

LARRY S. ROSEN
Celebration Teaching Academy, Stetson University

BRUCE TAYLOR
University of Dayton

TWIN LIGHTS
PUBLISHERS, INC.

Values-Based Teaching Skills: Introduction & Implementation

Revised Edition of *Developing Human Values*

ISBN 1-885435-02-9

Book and cover design, layout and typography
Sharp Des!gns, Holt, MI

Printed in the United States of America

Twin Lights Publishers, Inc.
Ten Hale Street, Rockport, MA 01966
Telephone: (508) 546-7398
Facsimile: (508) 564-5803

Portions of the material in this book were first published in *The Development of Consciousness*, Paulist Press, *Value Development – A Practical Guide*, Paulist Press, © 1982 and in *Readings in Value Development*, Paulist Press, © 1982 and later in *Developing Human Values*, International Values Institute 1990. Materials have been expanded, updated and revised for incorporation into this book. Contributing authors to this edition are Rodney N. Hall and Loretta M. Wells of the Values Technology Institute and Marilyn A. Ross. Additional contributions are referenced in the text.

Contents

4

Introduction

THIS IS A BOOK for educators about self-awareness and personal growth, about feelings, attitudes, choices and skills, about relationships both in one's intimate circle and in the schools and other institutions of our society. It proceeds from a conviction that education, to be worthy of the name, must encompass attitudes and values as well as concepts and facts. No education is neutral. Values are implied in everything we do as educators—the books and materials we choose, the curricula we set up, the criteria we use for grading students and the criteria that govern teacher certification, hiring and promotion—to name just a few examples. In our schools, with all their possibilities and difficulties, teachers are faced with acute value dilemmas about what to do, what to be and what to support.

This book is intended to help teachers to clarify and develop their own values, to enable them to foster value development in their students and to become agents for positive change at a systems level.

Value development is at once theoretical and practical, cognitive and affective; it is concerned with all facets of the personality, and offers sets of skills which can be taught and learned in order to further the development of teachers and their students.

Section I deals with the basics of value development theory: the four phases of consciousness, the factors that enable individuals to move through the phases, the relation between values and skills, the application of value theory to educational leadership and to the development of a values based curriculum.

Section II presents a series of exercises in the four skill areas since skill development is crucial to making changes in behavior and values. The exercises are experiential, presenting the individual with new data about the self and practical ways of increasing one's Instrumental, Interpersonal, Imaginal and Systems skills.

Section III contains the Teacher's Journal, the definitions of the 125 values identified in the work of Dr. Brian Hall, and a bibliography. The Journal leads directly to value questions that teachers face in their daily lives and is designed to enable the individual teacher to create a personal value development plan.

How to Use This Book

While individuals can benefit from reading this material, the exercises have been designed for groups of teachers working together cooperatively. If you feel uncomfortable or unprepared to facilitate certain exercises, invite a trained group facilitator to work with you.

Exercises have been written to include the following components:

1. A statement of objectives, indicating the relationship of the exercise to the building of specific skills. In working with a group of teachers, it is important to provide a brief theoretical rationale for each exercise, since many teachers will not invest themselves in the learning experience unless their need for understanding its relevance is satisfied. Materials useful for this purpose will be found in the introductions to various sections and to some of the exercises.

2. An activity, involving teachers experientially. This emphasis on active participation in the learning process accords with the assumption that education has too often neglected the importance of discovering our own truths in favor of memorizing the "facts" put forth by others. Direct experiential learning becomes truly owned, or, as one student has said, "Feeling is believing."

3. An opportunity for sharing observations, feelings, reactions and insights with others in cooperative learning groups.

4. Discussion questions to sharpen observations and to stimulate reflection on the meaning of the exercise and its connection to other experiences and ideas. The approach is experiential. Since the model is essentially an action/reflection one, it becomes even more critical that facilitators review the exercises themselves before attempting them

with a group. Of course, the more fully facilitators grasp the conceptual framework contained in this volume, the more easily they will be able to focus specific exercises productively. The attitude of the facilitator sets the tone for the teachers. If you, as facilitator, do not really believe in the exercise, neither will the teachers. Your conviction and enthusiasm will carry the group along with you. However, it is also wise to avoid raising expectations too high. What you communicate, verbally and non-verbally, in the first few minutes is the single most important element in creating a group climate of openness and trust. Therefore:

* Pay attention to the physical set-up. If you want the group to interact, seating needs to be arranged around a table or in a circle so that everyone can see everyone else without having to turn around.

* If you want teachers to share with each other, person-to-person, it is usually helpful to establish a first name basis for everyone, including the facilitator.

* Be conscious of the inclusion dynamics in the first five minutes of a group meeting. It is often useful to use a simple warm-up exercise which requires each teacher to say a few words.

* If you want teachers to share their feelings honestly with the group, you will need to model this behavior by sharing your own feelings, especially with your own staff or colleagues.

* With just a few exceptions, there are no right or wrong answers to the exercises. The aim is to encourage people to voice what they perceive and feel.

* The more you can model the skills and the values, the better.

* In dealing with the development of Imaginal skills, it is particularly important to create a supportive atmosphere that gives encouragement to free associations and "wild" ideas. It is often difficult for teachers, accustomed to dealing with convergent thinking and with problems that have one correct solution, to cope with a range of divergent responses. You may need to deal with your own feelings about "losing control of your group." Remember that in brainstorming it is important to scrupulously avoid passing judgment on responses until the final phase of the process.

* While this book emphasizes participation of all teachers in the exercises, we recognize that a group sometimes contains an

uninterested individual who simply does not want to participate. Do not press such individuals—let them play observer roles. There may also be some over-participators who are looking for an artificial emotional stimulus through group activities. It is wise not to let such people dominate the group. Sometimes participation will become such a strong norm that the group may try to pressure an individual who is disturbed or in a panic at the thought of a particular exercise. Most teachers know their own limits. It is important to respect such individuals and to leave a face-saving way for them to bow out. One can always learn something by watching.

* One exercise at each meeting is all that most teachers can digest. Too many structured exercises, run one after another, tend to confuse the participants and to prevent learning from sinking in. It is very important to allow sufficient time for processing both feelings and learning. Encourage teachers to express and, if possible, to resolve any feelings that may have been evoked by the exercise.

* Although a trained facilitator is always useful to a group, in certain exercises we have made a point of listing the facilitator as a necessary resource for a given exercise. In a few cases, such as brainstorming, some previous experience greatly increases the productivity of the exercise. However, in most cases, in listing the trained facilitator we wish to alert the user that the exercise is apt to lead into an emotionally charged situation. It is therefore necessary that the facilitator be experienced enough to aid members both to express their feelings and to come to a degree of closure with the episode.

* Ask the teachers to give you feedback on the usefulness of the experience, either through the use of simple, anonymous reaction sheets, or through a closure circle in which each teacher voices one positive and one negative evaluation of the session. Such feedback can be very useful in enabling you to adjust future presentations to make the exercises more dynamic, relevant and helpful.

Cooperative Learning Groups

The exercises in this book call for teachers to form cooperative learning groups. It is important, therefore, to be aware of the following differences between traditional groups and cooperative groups:

The following is taken from *Circles of Learning* by David Johnson, Roger Johnson, and Edith Johnson Holubec and describes the difference between traditional groups and cooperative groups. It is revised and used with their permission.

- Cooperative learning groups are based on positive interdependence among group members with goals structured in such a way that the teachers need to be concerned about each other's performance.

- In cooperative learning groups, there is clear individual accountability where each individual's mastery of the material is assessed, each group member is given feedback on her/his progress, and the entire group is given feedback about the progress of each member so that the other group members know whom to help and encourage. In traditional groups, individuals are not often held individually accountable for providing their share of the group's work.

- In cooperative learning groups, the membership is typically heterogeneous in ability and personal characteristics while traditional groups are often homogeneous in membership.

- In cooperative learning groups, all members share responsibility for undertaking leadership roles, while in traditional learning groups a leader is often appointed and given charge of the group.

- In cooperative learning groups, responsibility for each other's achievement is shared. In traditional learning groups, members are seldom held responsible for each other's learning.

- In cooperative learning groups, members' goals focus on maximizing each member's learning and maintaining good working relationships among members. In traditional learning groups, members often focus only on completing the assignment.

- In cooperative learning groups, the interpersonal skills on which members need to work collaboratively (such as leadership, communication, trust building, and conflict management) are directly taught, whereas in traditional learning groups these skills are assumed.

- When cooperative learning groups are used, the facilitator observes the groups, analyzes the problems they have working together and gives feedback to each group. In traditional learning groups, observation and intervention seldom take place.

* In cooperative learning, the facilitator structures procedures for groups to "process" how effectively they are working, while in traditional learning groups no processing takes place.

The following summarizes the difference between cooperative learning groups and traditional learning groups.

Cooperative Learning Groups	Traditional Learning Groups
Positive interdependence	No interdependence
Individual accountability	No individual accountability
Heterogeneous	Homogeneous
Shared leadership	One appointed leader
Shared responsibility for each other	Responsibility only for self
Interpersonal skills taught	Interpersonal skills ignored
Facilitator observes and intervenes	Little observation; no intervention
Groups process effectiveness	No group processing

Values and Teachers

Values and Teachers

THE FOUR PHASES OF CONSCIOUSNESS

V ALUES CAN BE classified into four significantly distinct phases of consciousness. Each phase of consciousness has its own world view which is determined by three factors: (1) how the world is perceived by the individual; (2) how the individual perceives the self functioning within that world; and (3) what human needs the self seeks to satisfy. Put another way, the self will function in response to the perceived pressures imposed by the external environment and in response to the felt human needs that impel from within. When the perceived environmental expectations change, and when the inner felt needs of the individual change, then the behavior of the individual changes. Implicit in an individual's behavior are the values that motivate and give priority to her/his activities, and the skills associated with the experience of successful performance. Briefly, then, this theory of consciousness and value development implies that the acquisition of quite specific skills is associated with each phase of consciousness. It also implies that quite specific human values can be associated with each of the four phases. The theory of consciousness development is descriptive, not prescriptive. It arises from observation and experience. Each phase can be easily described and readily understood by an ordinary observer of human behavior.

These phases can be identified in the natural pattern of growth from childhood through maturity. They can be identified in the history of a people or in the development of an institution or a culture. To say that the phases of

ELEMENTS	PHASE I	PHASE II	PHASE III	PHASE IV
How the WORLD is perceived by the individual	The world is a MYSTERY over which I have NO CONTROL	The world is a PROBLEM with which I must COPE	The world is a PROJECT in which I can PARTICIPATE	The world is a MYSTERY for which WE CARE
How the individual perceives its SELF to FUNCTION in the world	The self EXISTS at the center of HOSTILE WORLD	The self DOES things to succeed and to belong in a SOCIAL WORLD	The self ACTS on the CREATED WORLD with conscience and independence.	Selves GIVE LIFE to the GLOBAL WORLD
	Ego: self-centered	"They"	"I" as creative	"We"
What HUMAN NEEDS the self seeks to satisfy	The self seeks to satisfy the PHYSICAL NEED for food, pleasure and shelter	The self seeks to satisfy the SOCIAL NEED for acceptance, affirmation, approval, achievement	The self seeks to satisfy the PERSONAL NEED for being one's self, directing one's life, owning one's ideas	Selves seek to satisfy the COMMUNAL NEED for global harmony
BASIC VALUES	Safety/survival Security Sensory pleasure/ sexuality wonder/awe/fate	Family/belonging Competence/ confidence Self-worth	Independence Rights/respect Creativity Service/vocation	Health/healing Synergy Inter-dependence
Locus of Control	External Authority		Internal Authority	

Fig. 1

consciousness are developmental means that their sequence is ordered and irreversible. Each phase covers a larger space than the last one, because our awareness of the world around us expands as we become more conscious (*Values Shift*, by Brian P. Hall, p. 43). The person must satisfactorily experience each phase as an essential prerequisite for imagining the possibility of and then moving into a subsequent phase. However, an individual who has experienced a subsequent phase of consciousness may be forced, by the oppressiveness of the environment or by personal anxiety, to readopt behavior characteristic of an earlier phase.

Phase I normally corresponds to the first stage of development of a young child, taking into account both maturity and skills. A child normally passes beyond this phase by the age of six. People usually cannot move out of the second phase until they are at least sixteen. It would be unusual for anyone to reach to the fourth phase before the age of forty.

In the following sections, the phases of consciousness will be described in terms of their general characteristics and includes their perceptions of the world, their images of the self, and their felt human needs.

Phase I: The World As Mystery/The Self As Center

The Child

The world in Phase I is perceived as a mystery over which the individual has no control. For the newborn child it is "a big buzzing, booming confusion," unpredictable, changing, full of surprises. Moreover, it is peopled by giants on whom the child is totally dependent and over whom she or he has no control. The self struggles to exist in this capricious, perhaps hostile environment.

Babies live in a baby-centered world. Their perspective is egocentric, seeing the whole world as there just for them. A scene in A. A. Milne's *Winnie the Pooh* typifies this stage.

The little round bear is hungry and is looking for his favorite meal— honey. He looks up and sees a bee. He says to himself, "If I follow the bee to the tree, I will find honey for me." Winnie then goes on to conclude that there is honey in the tree, because he likes honey. "The honey must be there for me." As the story proceeds the little bear climbs up the tree and of course gets stung by the bee and has to run for his life.

This story depicts what we mean by the self-centered act. The self as center here does not mean that the individual is selfish in any moral sense; rather it indicates that the person sees the world as created for the self. Winnie the Pooh concluded that because there was a tree with honey and because he liked honey, it all must have been for him!

A similar experience familiar to many of us is that of going into a friend's house with a small child who then helps himself to the candy on the table. The child does not think this is wrong. Because there is candy in the house and he likes candy, it must be for him. At the age of two or three, this is not a moral question or a question of bad discipline, but rather a fact of the limited consciousness of the child. In the small child's view of the world, a lake may be defined as "the place where I go in the summer."

While the child is need-oriented, very physical and totally dependent, she/ he also responds to the beauty of this mysterious new world with wonder and awe.

This world of wonder and mystery where attention spans are short and nothing is really threatening is the world of innocence. This is a world, incidentally, that has often been carried into the adult world. We should be reminded, however, that such innocence, while suitable in the child becomes a problem for an adult.

The Adult

The power center for adults as well as for a child at this first level of consciousness is outside the self. Needs are dominant in determining one's behavior. An adult on this level may freely consent not to follow impulse, but is so influenced by these egocentric impulses that such resistance is rare. The person has few skills, either personal or environmental. As a result, the choices of an adult on this level focus on survival, security and physical pleasure. As a self-centered being, the person is aware primarily of the self and its preservation. When individuals at this level are not being threatened, they are aware of the self and its satisfaction. That drive for satisfaction becomes visible in curiosity and wonder and the need for physical affection.

Many of our modern adventure movies, such as the Indiana Jones and James Bond films, are built on the psychology of Phase I attitudes toward life. The keynotes of a good adventure movie are romance as physical affection, danger and survival. Overcoming one's enemy and gaining security are what give a sense of accomplishment to our heroes.

The struggle to survive in an alien hostile world can also be illustrated by real life episodes. The American frontier was pushed westward by people who perceived the wilds of the West and wiles of its Indians as enemies to be conquered. The robber barons of American industry waged economic war in their fight to the financial "top." Jews who survived the German "Holocaust" suffered the ignominious, even demonic effort to eliminate a race or to reduce its living members systematically to the tragedy and horror of a Phase I existence. Living in the Uganda of Idi Amin, in Kuwait under Saddam Hussein, in American slums, and in too many inner-city schools, persons experience Phase I consciousness and evidence corresponding behavior.

Phase I behavior, however, is not limited to persons confined to obviously oppressive environments. Much American advertising appeals to adults who buy products based on Phase I values. Sex images, totally irrelevant to the quality of the product, "sell" most cigarettes, much liquor and many automobiles.

Conclusion

The Phase I world view is centered around:
1. Self in its need for basic sense gratification
2. Self in its need for preservation
3. Self as innocent and without skills

The need for meaning at this level is tied to the need for survival and security. Anything that contributes to the satisfaction of the basic needs is a value to a person at this level—food, warmth, affection and the parent who supplies these things. Goals are immediate and concrete. Activity involving others tends to be manipulative, as of the child when needing to be fed. Even the exploratory activity of the child in response to a sense of wonder tends to be egocentric.

Most of the conflict in the child's life results from the fact that in reality the world is not just there for the child, but is for others as well; for example, a mother's involvement in other things of interest to her prevents her from responding to the child's every need or desire. Or the child encounters another child who takes away a favorite toy. These are the growth experiences that aid the child in moving to the next level where the world is now seen as there for others too.

Adults still functioning largely at this phase view things egocentrically. Intellectually, they may be aware that the world is there for others too, but they do not let that awareness interfere with their need-oriented behavior. They tend to deal with others in a manipulative way by being insensitive to others' needs. In this regard they differ from the child only in that their manipulative skills are superior.

Humans, however, are rational, intelligent beings. They differ from the animals in that as consciousness develops, they are able to recognize that survival requires getting along with others. They can move beyond the physical realm to a level of social accommodation.

Phase II: The World As a Problem/The Need for Belonging

At this phase the person sees the world as a problem to be solved. The basic problem that human beings face as they attain this level of consciousness is how to get on in the world—how to belong and how to acquire the skills necessary to be accepted and succeed.

The World of "THEY and THEM"

This phase of consciousness then is an extension of the first phase, but from self-preservation in a hostile world, the person moves to the problem of coping with a social world and winning the approval of important others. This is the world of the child five or six years of age and up. The world is seen by this person as being controlled by others. In the case of the child, "they" tend to be parents and teachers. As the person grows older, the adult at this phase will see "them" as being the politicians, the employers, the bishops—those in "authority." To be a successful person, therefore, one needs "their" approval.

It takes little imagination for a person to realize that the best way to win "their" approval is to acquire the skills and the self-competence that school, society and parents expect.

The World as Social

A central characteristic of consciousness at Phase II is that the person's world is enlarged beyond self-centered needs to include the social dimensions of life. The world is now there for others as well as for self; in fact a major constituent of the world is the way it is perceived by others, both by individuals, and, at a later stage, by institutions. The world that enters consciousness is one established by others into which the individual must fit in order to experience a sense of personal worth.

The infant joins his social world by winning the approval of his parents and the acceptance of his family. As a small child he begins to venture out of "the home" onto "the block," then into "the neighborhood" and finally into school where he learns to read, to write and to do arithmetic—the basic skills upon which personal competence and success will be built in "society." What the child learns to do in order that he might belong varies radically across cultures, but basically the socialization process follows a similar pattern of (1) identifying with significant groups and (2) adopting behavior— learning skills—expected of their members by those groups.

As the middle-class American child grows, membership increases—Little League, Brownies, Cub Scouts and 4-H Clubs. Associated with school life are a variety of extra-curricular group activities—most typically organized sports. These organized activities share two characteristics in common: (1) to belong, the youngster must live or play by the rules and (2) to succeed, the youngster must demonstrate personal achievement. Belonging and success are celebrated in initiation rites and rites of passage, both secular and sacred, often through induction ceremonies such as graduations and confirmations.

The Centrality of Self-Esteem

The central reference point in Phase II consciousness arises from the basic need for self-esteem, which is achieved by becoming useful as a participant in the regular activity of the existing order. Belonging and being accepted by others are key values. The person organizes experiences around this need to achieve self-esteem by meeting the expectations of significant others: family, peers and established institutions. The pursuit of this central need gives life meaning and order.

William Glasser has organized a system of psychotherapy around this need factor and calls it "Reality Therapy." He speaks of the basic needs of the human being in the following manner: "The fulfillment of the physiological needs of food, warmth and rest are rarely the concern of psychiatry. Psychiatry must be concerned with two basic psychological needs: the need to love and be loved and the need to feel that we are worthwhile to ourselves and others. Helping patients fulfill these two needs is the basis of 'Reality Therapy.'"

Elsewhere, Glasser introduces this subject of basic needs: "Before discussing the basic needs themselves, we must clarify the process through which they are fulfilled. Briefly we must be involved with other people, one at the very minimum, but hopefully many more than one. At all times in our lives we must have at least one person who cares about us and for whom we care ourselves."

Playing by the Rules

In the world perceived as established and run by others, a person must play by the accepted rules in order to be successful in the eyes of others. Not the least of those rules is that everyone must contribute in a productive way to society's well-being. In this regard, the person feels the need to develop appropriate skills and to engage in a useful and marketable activity.

The combination of the approval of significant others and one's own awareness of being skilled produces a sense of self-worth. As in Phase I, power and authority are judged to reside primarily outside the self in "them."

Skills for Growth

The person at this phase is still in a dependent relationship to the environment, but begins to seek control over it, through work, by developing the appropriate skills. Meaning now is not acquired through the satisfaction of the senses, but rather through an experience of working with others that is reinforced through social approval. Thus, a child goes to school where in a secure setting good behavior is rewarded. At that same time, skills are taught, enabling the individual to become competent and to cope with and manage the environment on one's own. Thus, work as productive labor is a high value at this stage. Work makes a person feel useful and provides one with the conviction of having earned the right to belong.

There is a potential danger at this phase of consciousness in that a person who lives in a society that reinforces the kinds of values typical of Phase II may fail to reach the next phase. In other words, if too much emphasis is placed on success and producing results, a person may conclude that self-worth comes only from work. This kind of distortion sees competence in work as the only way to achieve a sense of belonging. Our society, through its advertising and the Protestant work ethic, has emphasized the importance of work and success. It is important that we equally emphasize the other values in education and child rearing.

At this level, people see increasing significance in place and space. Social and work space are especially important, as is institutional space. Sacred space, at least at the ritual stage, is generally prized because it represents institutions that are concerned with one's sense of self-esteem. In many churches, the sense of belonging is a major outcome of the Sunday morning service.

Initially, people at this phase devote themselves so totally to learning how to attain a sense of self-esteem and competence in the world as established by others that they have little time or interest in considering alternatives to the existing order. However, once their skills enable them to feel at home in the present order, they are free to contemplate alternatives to the world as constituted. They are then ready to consider a move to the next phase.

Persons who have minimally satisfied the need to cope with the social environment begin to seek for meaning elsewhere. It is this process which leads them into the third phase of consciousness, where they experience the need to move beyond the requirement of "they" to independent actions, to making their own choices and decisions.

Phase III: The World As Project and Invention

We human beings are meaning hungry. As Philip Phenix writes in *Realms of Meaning*: "The fundamental human motivation is the search for meaning ... [The human being] can never rest content simply with biological satisfactions. He is forever disturbed by needs that are alien to animal existence. His real longing is for meaning, and whether he recognizes it or not, his striving, whatever its apparent object, is directed towards the enlargement and deepening of meaning."

It is quintessentially human to seek a conception of the universe and our place in it, a place that makes sense and gives meaning, dignity and purpose to our days. We have said that the phases are developmental. As in Abraham Maslow's hierarchy of needs, needs which are securely met no longer give meaning; values which are fully internalized no longer motivate. So long as the individual is engaged in a struggle to survive, self-preservation and security will dominate consciousness and give purpose to life. Once physical needs are met, people look for social acceptance, but once a person has internalized the value of self-worth, she/he begins to be less dependent on affirmation by others.

At the beginning of Phase III, living up to the expectations of others assumes less importance than being what I myself want to be. Internal and personal expectations replace external ones. The self begins to take charge. Doing something simply because another expects it or orders it ceases to be meaningful and is no longer a value around which to organize one's life. A personal sense of power and authority replaces institutional control or behavior. Consequently, creativity and imagination are prized. A new-found sense of honesty makes conformity hypocritical.

A person now becomes sensitive to the rights of others, acquires a concern for justice and literally expands the self into a larger society. Ira Progoff, writing in *The Symbolic and the Real* about Socrates, that great Greek figure who continually challenged the mind with his questioning, says of him in reference to his defense in the court at Athens before his final condemnation and death:

> Socrates there described his intimate feeling of why it was important for him to live his life as he had been living it. It was not a question of intellectual philosophy, but of a calling that came to him from two sources, an outward source and an inward source, which Socrates understood as ultimately not separate at all from one another.
>
> The outward source of his calling was the gods of the Greek Pantheon and to this the Oracle at Delphi testified. The inward source of his calling was the oracle within himself. He described this as the "divine faculty of which the internal oracle is the source." To Socrates, the inward and the outward were two aspects of a single principle. It was in the light of this unity that he could state his belief "that there were gods in a sense higher than any of my accuser's belief in them."

Progoff is speaking about that time in life when individuals have to be themselves, have to make statements because an inner voice calls them to a mission to be true to themselves rather than being guided by external voices in society or by the majority opinion. In terms of a phase of consciousness, we would say that the person can do no other because she or he has moved beyond the level that gave her or him meaning through the approval of others. Meaning is only present when the person listens to an inner voice. It is then at this point that Phase III consciousness develops for the first time. Figure 1 illustrates this in terms of the four phases.

In viewing the four phases of consciousness, we see a tremendous difference between the first two and the last two. Meaning for the first two comes basically from what is given from without. In the last two phases, authority is from within, and consequently what is meaningful to the person also comes from within.

We have to be careful here not to confuse internal authority with a lack of cooperation. Internal authority does not imply a radical independence in which one does not listen to any other individual, but only that one must consciously assume responsibility for the final decision oneself.

To actualize one's own being, the self in Phase III transcends its own limited world, becoming sensitive to the rights of all mankind. Liberation, freedom and independence become far more than matters for personal development. They become matters for group social action and national liberation. Thomas Jefferson clearly expressed this mentality over 200 years ago when he said that it was necessary for "one people to dissolve the political bonds which connected them with another" because they held the belief that life, liberty and the pursuit of happiness were inalienable rights. The Declaration of Independence illustrates a Phase III consciousness.

Many contemporary examples of Phase III behavior exist, but we need to make some distinctions. On the one hand, there are outstanding individuals whose personal concern for critical social and political issues is followed by responsible action, often at great cost. On the other hand, social action and political protest movements attract a variety of followers whose motivation and behavioral expression are nothing more than immature fadism or adolescent revolt. Suffice it to say that the late sixties and early seventies had their share of both types. Clearly, serious concern for the rights of minorities; efforts to eliminate the causes of poverty and institutional injustice; opposition to U.S. military intervention in Southeast Asia; active interest in conserving the sources of energy and preserving an ecological balance—all grew out of a Phase III consciousness. So do a variety of less visible expressions involving an individual life-style of dedicated service, creative imagination, high pain-tolerance, empathy, play and other activities where the person finds meaning in being oneself.

Phase IV: World As Mystery Cared For/Self As Life-Giver

At this phase, the person's world undergoes another expansion and enters consciousness as a series of interrelated tasks to be performed in conjunction with other like-minded people. There is complete transcendence of the self. The person now acts interdependently, in conjunction with other selves.

The person sees the world as unfinished, its present constitution not nearly as important as its future potentiality. This viewpoint implies no disregard or lack of concern for existing persons or communities, even though they too are viewed in their potentiality as much as in their actuality.

The world is seen as a mystery, but one for which human beings now take responsibility. We choose, create and enhance the environment. That is to say, we humans exercise authority over the world and work in a cooperative manner with each other and with nature itself in a common, interdependent action.

Global Transformation

At this phase of consciousness, the opposition between independent and interdependent action is no longer seen as valid. The transcendence of self involves a movement toward community. The reference point in consciousness, around which experience is organized, is a commitment to creative global transformation.

Global includes the "micro" as well as the "macro" system. In other words, the person's concern with such worldwide problems as poverty does not imply a lack of involvement with people on the local scene. On the contrary, this commitment to building a better world begins locally with the fostering of the spirit of mutual dedication among like-minded persons. The slogan holds: Think Globally, Act Locally.

Where independence was a primary value at Stage III, interdependence is primary here. Harmony and congruence are cherished as values in one's close personal relationships and in the cosmos as a whole. Another basic value is synergy, the conviction that several individuals may cooperate on a joint creative project with resulting effects that far exceed the sum of their individual efforts.

The harmonious balance envisioned in Phase IV seeks to see things in their wholeness and to understand the interrelatedness of parts (frequently opposing parts) to each other and to the whole. Understood in terms of Newtonian physics, harmony is seen as a state of equilibrium that can be achieved if we recognize the order of the universe and the mathematical laws that govern it. This view is characteristic of Phase II. Quantum physics, on the other hand, discounts the notion that reality is static, in a constant state of order and balance. Rather, it suggests that the opposite is the case. Understood in terms of quantum physics, harmony is seen in movement and tension, in the reconciliation of opposites. Congruence, or the suitable relatedness of things to each other and of parts to the whole, is essential to a Phase IV understanding of harmony.

The concept of harmony applies to the inner life of the individual as well as to the external world. Insights from Eastern religions and from depth psychology have raised in the Western mind a new awareness of the potential for personal harmony. At Phase IV, intimacy and solitude become unitive. However, the Phase IV person realizes that this harmony must be extended to technology and society and to the global community. Inner harmony must be integrated with social harmony through an appropriate technology. Ivan Illich's *Tools for Conviviality* (1973) suggests that man must be in control of his tools, of his technology, rather than be a victim of them. E. F. Schumacher's *Small Is Beautiful* (1973) suggests that we need to develop an intermediate technology that is congruent with the growth needs of the persons who use it. Convivial tools and intermediate technology both illustrate a Phase IV consciousness.

At Phase IV, then, the world is perceived as a mystery for which we, like-minded persons, must care. The world is perceived globally or holistically—the natural world, the human communities and persons who live in it, the technology that has transformed it. Within this global context, Phase IV selves seek to enliven, to nurture persons and communities from the context of consciousness that is meaningful to them. In doing so, the interdependent "we" responds to the common call to strive for global harmony, to build and to renew the face of the earth.

Growing Phase-Wise

The four phases of consciousness we have just described must be understood before we can go more deeply into the question of valuing, for these world views open up or limit the values we can choose and the manner in which we define them. At every phase of development, the need for meaning is central, but at each phase it is tied to different concrete needs. For our purposes, this is of great importance, since nothing can qualify as a value that does not contribute to one's meaning system.

Meaning and consciousness then are interrelated. Individuals find meaning as they develop values that allow them to feel at home in the world. The values they choose and the manner in which they define them are rooted in their phase of consciousness. As women and men move through the phases of consciousness and seek to find meaning, their struggles involve two basic operations: (1) exploration and (2) integration.

Exploration and Integration

One of the basic tasks for anyone trying to promote human growth is to find ways of fostering the human ability first to explore and then to integrate new situations successfully so that they feel at home in the newly encountered world. In the birth experience itself, the child moves from the comfortable environment of the womb into an external environment which immediately places new demands upon it. Its needs are no longer met automatically. As the parent touches, cuddles and cares for the infant, it begins to explore and integrate the environment, to feel comfortable in it.

If the process of integration is not achieved, growth is impossible. That is why the environment in the home and classroom is so important for the young child. It must be one that fosters curiosity, gives the freedom to explore, and yet does not overwhelm the child with so many alternatives that she or he is unable to control and integrate what is found.

Human life cannot be meaningful if it is not at the same time purposeful and directed toward goals. The absence of purpose in the adult, especially long-range purpose, slowly renders the person rudderless and without meaningful criteria to guide the making of choices. It is purposeful behavior that gives human life order. Without it, life would be just a series of episodes not integrated into any meaningful pattern.

VALUE DEVELOPMENT

The Nature of Values

Values are the driving forces which motivate us as human beings. They are ideals that shape and give significance to our lives (*Values Shift*, by Brian P. Hall, p. 2). They are reflected through the priorities that we choose, the decisions we make and actions we take. Values are the consciously or unconsciously held priorities that both shape and reflect the world view of an individual or an institution. The phrase "world view" is another way of saying "the way we see the world through our values" (*Values Shift*, p. 43). Values combine to form one's world view and one's world view gives shape to one's values. It is a reciprocal effect—the one reinforces the other.

Values, then, are the mediators between our inner world—our hopes, ideals, dreams and images—and the external and observable world of everyday life and human behavior. Our values stand between the two worlds, and are a way of understanding both our inner life and our external behavior (*Values Shift*, p. 35). This underlying concept of values theory is based on an ancient idea that only recently has been confirmed by modern research.

Based on research by Brian Hall of Santa Clara University, 125 value words have been identified in written and spoken language that consistently appear throughout the life span of individuals and organizations. These value words appear to be stable and evident across all social strata, languages and cultures. (These 125 value words and their definitions are listed in the back of this book.)

Values come out of a phase of consciousness but are expressed through specific behaviors. Thus in the diagram below, the individual who is fearful that he may be robbed buys a handgun to protect himself and his valuables, acting out a Phase I consciousness.

Conversely, from the behavior, we may discern the values and phase of consciousness of an individual. Let us see how this works in a specific example.

A Case Study

Sally Forth is a teacher in a high school near Orlando, Florida. We see her as she arrives home after a staff meeting which has just ended. Her primary interest at this time is to be accepted as a successful, competent individual. She is concerned about the image she conveys to people, the clothes she wears, the conversational skills she demonstrates. She wonders if she has upset anyone at the meeting. She decides, after reflection, that she probably

PHASE	WORLD VIEW	EXAMPLES OF BEHAVIOR	VALUES
I	World as Alien Mystery	Buys handgun Installs alarm system	Self-Preservation Security
II	World as a Problem of Belonging	Tries to make good impression Earns good grades	Self-Worth Self-Competence
III	World as an Inventive Project	Begins new business Organizes campaign for affordable housing for poor people	Independence New Order
IV	World as a Mystery to be Cared For	Works for UN agency Joins medical team in third world country to bring service to remote areas	Interdependence Rights/World Order

Fig. 2

carried it off pretty well. We can guess that Sally is operating at Phase II. Her focus is on what others think of her and whether or not she "belongs." She achieves a sense of meaning to her life if others see her as a prestigious individual.

We next see Sally working busily at her computer. It is past ten in the evening. She has a telephone supported by her shoulder while at the same time she is writing lesson plans on the computer. We have enough information about Sally's behavior to make inferences about her value priorities, but behavior choices are not values in themselves, they are, rather, "value indicators." The indicators are the primary materials for value development diagnosis.

Sally's late night energies reveal the following values *(See Values Definitions, pp. 151 ff.)*:

1. Work/Labor
2. Economics/Success
3. Achievement/Success

She could probably rank them in a different order. The world view or phase does not determine the rank order, but it does limit the values she can perceive as meaningful. In order to confirm Sally's value configuration, we need to make sure that she has defined the above values in about the same way as we have defined them. What makes this process of value discovery complex is that Sally, depending on her phase of consciousness, might define "work" in a different way. At Phase I, Sally might be working merely to get enough bread on the table and thus "working" would merely be an indicator linked to the underlying value of Self-Preservation. At Phase III, Sally may regard teaching as a service opportunity she has chosen as the best way for her to contribute to society. Teaching would then be linked to the underlying value of Service.

Let us take another example of how value indicators must be analyzed in order to discover their underlying values. When asked why she worked, Sally might have replied, "To earn money ... doesn't everybody?" The word "money," however, is not itself a basic value within our model. Sally obviously is not likely to value dollar bills or coins for their own sake unless she is a collector and interested in their aesthetic value. If you asked her, "Why do you value money?" she might reply, "I need protection from disasters I can't foresee," or, "I want to save for the house my fiancé and I plan to buy," or "I really want that new car." By the use of value clarification methods, Sally would be encouraged to identify values from the list of 125 values which would then give a clearer picture of Sally's phase of consciousness.

Once the values have been derived from the experience, as illustrated in Sally's case, we then suggest that the person choose four or five values and rank them in order of priority, as they most closely represent day-to-day behavior. (See Teacher's Journal.) The reason for this procedure is that behavior, the stance of the self to the environment, is always a matter of values ranked in a particular order. It is never a matter of a single value in isolation. Sally might, for example, with respect to the indicator, money, have chosen the following ranking:

1. Prestige/Image
2. Achievement/Success
3. Leisure

One can see that this ranking will lead to a certain kind of behavior. The person who places Prestige or Achievement first is going to behave quite differently from a person who puts Leisure first. Again, it is important that Sally and others involved in this clarification process define the values in the same way.

Often people will find that their definitions of the 125 values are different from our standardized ones. They are then asked to choose a more appropriate value to express what they mean. For example, some who have chosen Prestige might decide that they really meant Competence. Some may confuse Security with Belonging or Self-Worth with Self-Actualization or Being Self. An important point to remember is that when values are defined subjectively, based on one's own personal experience rather than using the standard definitions, the value changes its definition at each phase of consciousness. Education for a small child at Phase I is merely going to school because a parent desires that behavior. One goes simply out of love or fear of punishment. At Phase II, Education is something one does at school in order to earn good grades to get a diploma. At Phase III, Education is an experience enjoyed for its own sake, and at Phase IV may simply mean intuitive insight. While Education in all four phases shares the common definition of gaining new knowledge, the meaning for individuals will shift depending on the world view of each.

The process of moving from the specific behaviors to discerning the values and phase of consciousness then involves the following steps:

1. Examining a particular set of behaviors
2. Drawing out the underlying values from the value indicators
3. Choosing several of those values and ranking them so as to describe the behavior in terms of the values
4. Taking each of those values, defining them in terms of personal experience and then lining up that definition with the standardized definition from the list of 125 values
5. Looking over these new definitions and, in light of the revised understanding, choosing new values, if necessary, and reordering the values

Moving Through the Phases

Each value priority can be related to the skills that enable us to develop it in our lives. Thus the value of Care/Nurture requires the skills of awareness of another's needs, hearing the thoughts and feelings of another accurately, interpreting non-verbal communication accurately, being able to hold and cuddle another.

What makes people grow? There are four basic conditions for healthy growth:

1. The person needs the basic values and the minimal skills to actualize those values at each phase of development
2. The person must be in an environment—in family, school, work place, larger community—that reinforces the values of the present stage of development
3. The environment must also offer challenges to growth, that is, examples of behavior that embodies values of the next phase of development

4.   Persons need to know themselves well enough to identify values and
     skills they do not yet have but need in order to grow

Phase I

In simple terms, newborn children, in order to grow, must first experience
an environment that allows them to preserve their physical existence without
threat. Once children have received the love, kindness and care from their
parents (or other primary caretaker) that make them feel physically protected,
then Self-Preservation and Security will no longer be predominant needs
for them, even though Security will always be a primary value in their lives.
Even in a crisis situation, Self-Preservation will not require constant attention
and worry if they have experienced early in their life an environment which
allowed them to internalize a sufficient "basic trust."

The basic environmental condition for the reinforcing of values at this
level is the experience of love from others and an external environment that
is not frightening, but rather can be relied on to meet one's needs. It is important that the environment be reasonably responsive to the child's demands. By
"environment" here we mean the home, the classroom, and later the workplace.

Children whose cries rarely meet with a response are apt to experience
their environment with distrust. Children who are spoken and sung to, played
with, held by several different people, tend to develop better and more quickly
than those deprived of interaction.

Phase II

What gives young people meaning at Phase II is belonging to the social world.
They turn to their peers, to their friends, and begin to socialize. Their
consciousness has changed, thus they require new skills and begin the process
of internalizing new values. In order to go through the second phase, they
must eventually internalize the values of Self-Worth and Competence.

Self-Worth is the internalization of the conviction that one is of value to
others as well as to oneself. It is the feeling that one is intrinsically good.
Within religious experience—particularly in the Christian and Jewish
traditions—it is the affirmation that God sees human beings as good and
that creation itself is good. We may act badly at times, but still we are
intrinsically good. To understand this and to adhere to this belief is to have
internalized a sense of Self-Worth.

Competence is an extension of Self-Worth and means that one knows oneself to be competent as an individual and possessed of sufficient Instrumental and other skills to be of use to others and to oneself within society. It is a sense of adequacy. It is the opposite of the feeling of inadequacy and powerlessness. It is one's awareness that one can begin and finish a job well.

The two values that we have just defined are critical to modern education. The purpose of education, as we know it, is twofold. We must instill in young people a sense of their own value, while at the same time preparing them to be competent to go out and earn a living and make a contribution to the world and society. The school environment necessary for these values to be internalized is an environment that affirms the individual so that she or he grows up with a sense of Self-Esteem, rather than with a feeling of inadequacy or inferiority.

It is the job of education through all the grade levels to make these values a conscious reality for the child. The job of the teacher is to make the child aware of these values as soon as possible so that each child can internalize them and can also be urged to create environments which help other people to realize these values. A child who has a sense of Self-Worth or Self-Esteem must be taught how to behave so as to affirm the Self-Worth of others. That is to say, every value has two dimensions to it: the experience of the value from others, and, the ability to affirm that value in others.

Phase III

At the end of Phase II, a radical change takes place as a person has the opportunity to move from Phase II to Phase III. The reinforcing environment that allows a person to internalize values at this level must be one that encourages Independence and Responsibility.

The values in Phases I and II are what Abraham Maslow called D-Cognition values ("D" for "deficiency"). Psychologists generally consider these values as absolutely necessary for physical and mental health. Almost all social work and counseling practice is directed toward the building of these D-Cognition values in individuals in order for them to function happily and productively in society. The values in Phase III and IV are called growth values or what Maslow termed B-Cognition ("B" for "being") values. An important starting point in the growth area is the value of Independence.

Independence, according to the *Oxford Unabridged Dictionary*, is "the condition or quality of being independent; the fact of not depending on another [with various shades of meaning]; exemption from external control or support; freedom from subjection or from the influence of others; individual liberty of thought or action."

Being Self is the quality of being oneself while actualizing being in others. It is the experience of having been sufficiently independent to move to the point where one can create more and more experiences in the world that reinforce environments that allow others to become themselves also. Being Self is different from Independence in that it has the added quality of making one's presence felt in society.

The reinforcing environment for this kind of development comes primarily from one's peers, who, as fellow journeyers, share the same wish to be self-actualized. We are essentially stating that at this stage, unlike the first two stages, dependence on the external environment has become a secondary rather than an essential condition for growth. It is necessary, therefore, that a person be in an external environment that permits the individual to be independent in the first place.

Such an environment is one that is reinforced by persons who have actualized the value of Being Self. In other words, the environment is one of freedom which permits a person to make mistakes and to grow in responsibility. The individual learns from those mistakes as much as from doing things correctly all the time—something that would upset a person emphasizing Competence.

Phase IV

An important value in Phase IV is Interdependence. Interdependence is seeing and acting on the awareness that personal and inter-institutional cooperation are always preferable to individual decision-making.

Synergy is a particularly important form of Interdependence. By Synergy we mean the cooperative action of discrete agents, such that the total effect is greater than the sum of their effects taken separately. In Synergy, the whole cannot be predicted from the parts; rather, many interdependent entities come together to form a new and transcendent whole. Thus, four people come together with four different ideas; as they work, they produce a new idea that was originally unknown to any of them. Briefly put, in Synergy, the whole is greater than the sum of its parts.

The environment that reinforces the development of these values is a highly developed state of reality in which individuals operate together interdependently. There is a community with a lifestyle that allows the members to act in a harmonious manner with the total environment, reinforcing it and one another.

As individuals, we might have difficulty in understanding this advanced phase of consciousness. Still, these values become need values for the individuals operating at Phase III and moving toward Phase IV.

The Role of the Teacher in Value Development

As individuals grow older, they tend to move toward greater maturity, but the process is by no means automatic. Each new stage presents aspects of both attraction and repulsion: the person wants to grow, to expand, to try the new skill or behavior but at the same time fears the risk involved in possible failure. Witness the baby learning to walk, the young person making a first speech in public, the adolescent on a first date. What can the teacher do to promote growth and help students to internalize values in an authentic way? All of us have no doubt experienced the failure of straightforward indoctrination, reinforced by a system of rewards and punishments. Children required by their parents to attend church every Sunday may never darken the door of a church in their adult lives.

We seem to be impaled on the horns of a dilemma: on the one hand, values seem to be caught rather than taught; on the other hand, it is impossible for education to be value neutral. Fostering value development in one's students is rather like gardening. The gardener cannot make the seed grow; the teacher cannot make the child internalize values. The gardener provides a nurturing environment—a seed bed, fertilizer, moisture, sunshine, a stake if necessary, some pruning. Similarly, the teacher provides a nurturing environment.

There are five main ways in which the teacher can foster value development:

1. First of all, the teacher can provide an environment that reinforces the student's present stage of growth. The basic values of each phase must be fully internalized before the person can move on to the next phase. Once values are fully internalized, the person is likely to search for new sources of meaning and value. The person who is secure in Belonging and Self-Worth, key values of Phase II, is apt to take the risks involved in Independence and Creativity, key values of Phase III.

2. The teacher can foster self-awareness in students, promoting value clarification and reflection to help students identify their present phase with its foundation, focus and future values.

3. The teacher can expose students to role models, concrete examples—
    from literature, history, the local community or the national news—
    of persons acting out of values at the next stage. Value development is
    like walking along a winding road. At Phase I, the individual literally
    is unable to perceive Phase III values, just as the traveler cannot see
    what is around the bend. By using examples, the teacher can fire the
    imagination with future values.

4. The teacher's own person is a powerful role model. It is important for
    the teacher to be honest about his or her own feelings and values and
    to be willing to admit mistakes and limitations. Teachers are not called
    to be perfect, just honest.

5. The teacher can provide training in relevant skills. Skills are, by
    definition, teachable; they can be learned by practicing under
    supervision. Acquiring the necessary skills and practicing the related
    behaviors open the way to internalizing the values. We cannot teach
    caring, but we can teach attentive listening, how to read non-verbals,
    perception checking, reflecting the other's feelings—all skills that
    enable one to enter the world of the other.

VALUES AND SKILLS

A major key to the process of value development for teachers is the acquisition of the requisite skills. Behind every value is an inventory of skills. A value can only be expressed in behavior to the extent that the person has developed the skills that the value requires. Thus, if the value "Trust" is to be expressed in one's behavior, then the person must have, as a minimum, the following skills: the ability to identify one's own feelings accurately, the ability to express one's feelings openly and appropriately, the ability to identify another's feelings and thoughts accurately.

Skills are acquired by repeated acts under the supervision of a competent coach. This process is especially clear in the case of such sensory motor skills as driving a car, playing tennis, typing, riding a bicycle. Generally, when we attempt to acquire a new skill, we go through the following stages:

1. *The unconscious incompetent.* We don't know and we are unaware of our ignorance. Thus, we may admire a fast game of tennis, but be unaware of different strokes and strategies involved in winning.
2. *The conscious incompetent.* We become aware of what is to be learned. We begin to see the skill in all its complexity and refinements.
3. *The conscious competent.* If we give full attention to the task, we are able to achieve the new behavior, to shift the gears smoothly and noiselessly, to hit the ball squarely in the center of the racquet. However, in a stressful situation, we will probably revert back to our old behavior.
4. *The unconscious competent.* The skill is fully internalized—we shift gears without thinking, we employ forehand and backhand with equal ease.

A similar process is involved in internalizing a value. The phase of consciousness limits the values an individual can perceive. Thus, a person at Phase I literally cannot see Phase III values; they are beyond her/his horizon. However, if a Phase II value presents itself in a concrete example, new aspirations may stir in the individual, who then becomes a conscious incompetent. Take the value of Order, for example. Under supervision, the adolescent may put her/his belongings in order. However, under pressure—when rushing to an exciting event—the individual will throw order to the winds. When the value is fully internalized (as it often is in medical or military personnel), strict order will be maintained, even in highly stressful situations. In short, the value will have become second nature.

In the process of internalization, values and skills are intimately related.

We begin to internalize the value by practicing the related skills. As I master my tools, I begin to take pride in my craftsmanship. As my skills increase, I perceive new possibilities, and my appreciation of good design and workmanship grows accordingly. The development of the skill leads to the internalization of the value. For the teacher seeking growth, it is crucial to understand this relation between skills and value development.

Foundation, Focus and Future Values

Another way to look at this process of development is in terms of Foundation, Focus and Future Values. Some of our values are more indicative of where we would like to be than where we actually are. These are our aspirations or Future Values. Other priorities are ones we are aware of, but for the most part, they are taken care of, fully internalized. These are our Foundation Values. In between our aspirations and our foundations are the values we are struggling to internalize. We call these Focus Values since they are the focus of our choices in day-to-day living. Empathy, for example, is a value we may be trying to implement but for which we need more skills. Focus Values are those which we can actualize when we are not under pressure. If we give full attention to the task, we are able to achieve the new behavior, e.g., to shift gears smoothly, to note the non-verbal signals. However, in a stressful situation, we will probably revert to our old behavior. As a person develops the skills related to Focus Values, these priorities tend to become internalized as Foundation Values, and the person will grow toward her/his aspirations or Future Values.

The Four Skill Areas

We can classify the myriad skills which human beings exercise under four main headings: (1) Instrumental skills, (2) Interpersonal skills, (3) Imaginal skills, and (4) Systems skills,

As we explore each of these areas in some detail, it will become apparent that there is some overlap from one area to another. Although the lines of division are not completely clear-cut, there is something distinctive about each skill area that makes this fourfold arrangement useful.

A look at child development shows us how closely the different skill areas are related. At birth, the human infant has the potential to develop all the skill areas. In the first year of life, the rudiments of the first three skill areas are already being laid down. Thus, the newborn begins immediately to develop Instrumental skills, e.g., the skills of grasping and holding onto an object, of turning over and sitting up, crawling, walking and talking. At almost the same time, for babies are born into a network of human relationships, the infant begins to respond to other people. The parents cuddle their offspring, speak or sing to the child, and soon are rewarded with a smile or a laugh. Long before they are a year old, most babies show signs of considerable interpersonal awareness and are quite skillful in making their needs known and getting them met.

Imaginal skills are present in germ in the childhood experiences of self-delight and wonder. They begin to develop as the child starts to draw, to build, to play "Let's pretend," but can only come to full development in Phase III when the autonomous individual values her or his creativity and expresses it freely. Systems skills are the last to develop, for they require all the other skills together with the ability to handle high levels of abstract analysis, to synthesize complex data from diverse sources and to project alternatives into a distant future.

Instrumental Skills

Instrumental skills are task-oriented. They encompass all the abilities that enable one to get a job done: that blend of intellectual and physical competencies that enable one to shape both ideas and the external environment. They include the skills involved in physical dexterity, handicrafts and cognitive accomplishments.

Entry Level Skills   Entry level skills are the general skills expected of members of a particular society without which the individual cannot be said to belong fully to the society. Without these basic entry level Instrumental skills, the achievement of a sense of Self-Worth will be severely limited.

These general skills represent the minimum expectations a society builds into its culture. In primitive societies, it is expected that every adult male will be able to hunt, fish, dance, sing and make weapons. Puberty rites are a kind of ritual certification that the initiates are qualified skill-wise to function as adult members of the tribe. Certification by a college degree or by successful completion of student teaching serves much the same function for teachers, though without the religious overtones of the primitive ritual.

In our society, with its many complex legal, financial and political systems having an impact on everyone's life, the "three R's" at a rather sophisticated level are entry-level skills. Persons who are functionally illiterate have a hard time surviving.

Professional and Specialized Skills   A sense of belonging and Self-Worth are also enhanced by the acquisition of more specialized skills. A teacher of history belongs to a very select group and can be confident that this peculiar specialty is not typical of the general populace. The same can be said of a plumber, a dentist or a certified public accountant.

Professional skills also empower a person to be more independent than others who must cope with life without these exceptional skills. The competence that professionals attain frequently frees them from the worries and concerns typical of those whose basic aim in life is to meet the expectations of others.

The Use of Tools in Human Development   The skill to use tools can be simple or a highly sophisticated art. As Ivan Illich indicates "I use the term 'tool' broadly enough to include not only simple hardware such as drills, pots, syringes, brooms, building elements or motors and not just large machines like cars or power stations. I also include among tools productive institutions such as factories, which produce tangible commodities such as cars and electric current, and production systems for intangible commodities such as 'education,' 'sick care,' 'conflict resolution' or which 'make' decisions. I use the term 'tool' for lack of any other term which would be equally general and simple."

Not everyone is equally qualified to use all the tools described by Illich. Phase IV persons must have the ability to design and use tools that meet the needs for construction of the ideal world as perceived in their vision of the future. This is beyond the reach of a person whose capabilities are strained by using a hammer or screwdriver or reading the newspaper.

For centuries, education has emphasized Instrumental skills as the key to what is human. Our growth in cognitive abilities, the application of thought to the making of tools, and the expansion of various personal skills constitute the history of the development of civilization. An Instrumental skill is the manner by which we utilize our tools. At one level an individual has skills in using a hammer. Hands and brain coordinate the maximum use of "the instrument called hammer." The skill, then, is a coordinating function. At a more sophisticated level, the principal of a school has "skills" in the use of the tool "management," coordinating budgets, teachers, and office staff and many other elements into a single efficient instrument.

Interpersonal Skills

Interpersonal skills equip persons to enter into deeply satisfying human relationships and to widen their circle of social relationships. They involve the ability to perceive self and others accurately and to communicate these perceptions in ways that facilitate mutual understanding, trust, cooperation and intimacy.

A high point of Interpersonal skills is the capacity for intimacy with another person. An intimate relationship is one in which I share my innermost being, my hopes and fears, anxieties and aspirations, my thoughts and emotions with another human being in such a way that I encourage her or him to feel free to do likewise. Obviously, such a relationship requires the skills of attentive listening and accurate communication of one's thoughts and feelings. These skills, basic to any human relationship, must be fostered at home and early in a child's school experience.

A most essential Interpersonal skill, and yet one often neglected, is the ability to get in touch with one's own feelings. Most people learn to express what they think about something—for example, about their mistreatment by someone. But how many people, in the face of mistreatment, are able to sort out and deal maturely with how they feel about such an experience? Until one can do this, one does not really know one's innermost being and therefore cannot share that inner self with another.

What lies behind these assumptions are the kinds of Interpersonal skills that must be acquired if the growth goal of intimacy is to become a real possibility. There is a correlation between a person's expansion of consciousness and the deepening and widening of social relationships. The ultimate in the "depth dimension" is the capacity to enter into intimate human relationships. The ultimate in the "breadth dimension" is to expand from the self-centered world of the child through the family, the neighborhood, the school, the work group and to see the whole human race as one's in-group. In order to move through these phases, the individual, at each stage, needs to acquire new Interpersonal skills as well as to intensify and deepen existing ones.

Imaginal Skills

A fertile imagination is an indispensable element in the acquisition and exercise of all the skills already considered. It takes imagination to design tools or to relate creatively to other persons.

The Structure of the Imagination   What we mean by the imagination is the synergetic interaction between fantasy, emotions and the reflective intellect of human beings. This process is synergetic—that is, it results in something new, a product which is greater than the sum of its constituent parts. New ideas emerge from data that has been gathered from the person's environment, evaluated, organized and reflected on constructively.

This explains why the imagination is so often described as the faculty that enables a person to see alternatives to reality as presently constituted.

The Complexity of the Imagination   The imagination does more than produce simple ideas. It also combines several ideas in order to form a hypothesis and then uses that hypothesis to examine new data to form a theory. Eventually, after sufficient testing of the theory, it may formulate a law like Newton's Law of Gravity.

Through Imaginal skills, human beings modify their external environment by applying ideas in creative (and unfortunately also in destructive) tool making. Imaginal skills apply equally to tools that modify the physical environment, tools that modify human beings and tools that enhance life.

In order for the imagination to be stimulated, basic need values such as security, approval and a sense of personal adequacy and worth have to be minimally satisfied. At this point, a person can begin to explore alternatives to his or her present lifestyle.

Stunting Imaginal Growth   It is not difficult to envision the kind of school environments that discourage Imaginal growth. Following is a list of factors that inhibit the development of the imagination:

- A teacher with a style of authority that creates dependency
- Teachers who discourage and even punish personal initiative
- An absence of challenges that involve problem solving
- Success stressed so much that fear of failure is strong, and initiative and experimentation discouraged
- An absence in school of learning the creative use of leisure—for example, poetry, fairy tales, travel and an appreciation of history and other cultures

Fostering Imaginal Growth   Among the characteristics of an environment that can encourage the imagination are the following:

- Teaching and leadership styles that encourage personal initiative

* Institutional frameworks: home and schools that foster minimal care, security and consistency
* Supportive teachers who challenge students and encourage them to risk
* Emphasis on student resourcefulness and experimentation which are rewarded even if they lead to failure
* A school where cultural differences are explored as a unique asset
* A school where group problem solving (brainstorming) is a frequent experience
* A school where honest self-expression and independence are valued

Imaginal Skills and Valuing   Valuing as a process is itself an Imaginal skill, a process of choosing from alternatives in one's life. It is only possible to choose from among alternatives if one can first imagine them together with their consequences. If Imaginal skills are to be balanced and healthy they must include the ability to:

* tolerate ambiguity
* play with a problem, redefining it from a fresh angle
* see connections between seemingly unrelated parts
* put existing data together in new ways
* elaborate an idea or a plan, developing details
* dream new futures
* use brainstorming techniques
* use many modes of communication, i.e., poetry, drama, visuals, gesture, movement

Systems Skills

Systems skills enable one to see the parts in relation to the whole. They include the ability to analyze a complex whole by identifying its parts, to grasp the inter-relationships among the parts, to plan interventions to change existing systems and to design new systems. Clearly, Systems skills depend upon the development and integration of the other three sets of skills, and therefore are the last to be fully developed.

As we progress through the phases of consciousness, our world expands, and we find ourselves confronted with more and more complexity in our lives. Children grow up learning to cope with the family system, then they have to learn to cope with the school system, where they must deal with classmates, teachers and administrators. Eventually, they move to the world of work where they must meet the expectations of a boss and co-workers.

Systems Skills and Development   An important point to understand is that what constitutes a skill at one stage of a person's development may become an impediment to growth at a later stage. For example, as one moves out beyond the family into society, initially one needs to learn to fit into that society and its systems. But if the basic concern, as one involves oneself in these systems, is only to conform or fit in, then growth will be delayed. What was a valuable skill and means for achieving a sense of belonging at one time has now become a liability. Passive responses should eventually give way to creative initiative and active responsibility.

A Case Study   We now need to take a look at some concrete examples of the relationship between the development of values and the acquisition of the four sets of skills. Let us look at a case study.

Lois was a principal of a 1,100-student middle school in a medium-sized city in eastern Wisconsin. She was experiencing loneliness and doubts about her Self-Worth as she was approaching retirement, and felt that her role as administrator in the school did not permit her to get to know people very well. During a consultation session, Lois was asked to describe how she saw herself and her life vocation.

Once she had described her situation, she was able to identify the underlying values that she said were representative of her own behavioral priorities. She listed them as follows:

1. Competence/Confidence
2. Achievement/Success
3. Independence
4. Self-Worth

As she described this ranking, she noted that Self-Worth was very important to her but was low on her list because of her sense of loneliness. She had gained a great deal of Self-Worth through her ability to achieve the job of principal and through her recognized competence in education. However, she also said that a high priority for her was Independence, but it was third on the list because running the school, which was the most important to her, made independent action difficult.

When she was asked how she would like these values to be prioritized in her behavior, she ranked them as follows:

1. Independence
2. Self-Worth
3. Competence/Confidence
4. Achievement/Success

Interestingly, she described Independence as being able to do some creative things on her own and to get to know new people. She felt that Self-Worth meant much to her because she was lonely and would like to have something in her life other than work. As we began looking at the situation, we recognized that, in her initial ranking that described her behavior, the first two values are from the second phase of consciousness but the last one is at the third phase.

When she described how she would like to be, the value that came from the third phase of consciousness (Independence) moved to first place. Reflecting on this situation, we might conclude that we have here a description of a person growing from one phase of consciousness to another.

As she described herself, she noted that she had a high sense of Competence and was, in fact, able to cope with the system of the school effectively. One would therefore assume that she would naturally move into the third phase of development. But as she herself noted, there was something that stopped her. An obvious conclusion was that it might have something to do with Self-Worth.

In order to see the developmental picture more clearly, we need to look at the four sets of skills. When Lois described her four values, she noted that she had excellent Instrumental skills but felt that she was not a very creative person and often had difficulty in relating to people. This made it evident that a lack of developed Interpersonal and Imaginal skills contributed to her diminished sense of Self-Worth. A program of development for her would have to help her structure her personal relationships so that her Self-Worth could be enhanced and would allow her to grow into another phase of development. In short, she needed to develop Interpersonal skills.

Lois really knew a great deal about the workings of the school, had no difficulty in talking to persons in authority and was able to get things done efficiently. In short, she had good Instrumental and Systems skills. Then, as is often the case, the system responded to her Systems skills and made her an administrator. But leadership that is interdependent and holistic requires more than Instrumental and basic Systems skills.

Without Imaginal skills a leader would not be able to move the system along, but would simply maintain what had been. This was the case with Lois. It is imagination that enables the leader to have vision. Then too because of her lack of Interpersonal skills, she tended to move the system along with a blatant disregard for the people involved. She did not dislike people; on the contrary, she simply lacked sufficient Interpersonal skills.

Leadership   The last example points to the minimal requirements that are necessary for a person in a leadership position. Obviously, the person who is placed at the head of a school has to have skills in planning and initiation. In terms of phases of development, this means that the person is minimally at the third phase of consciousness with the needed concomitant skills. Contemporary school culture requires at least that much.

In order to be a holistic leader, one has to have all four skill areas operating. The person must be able to move the organization with vision (Systems and Imaginal skills), and yet be able to deal with individuals in a caring manner (Interpersonal skills). At the same time, he or she must be able to deal with the system professionally (Instrumental skills).

Lois's difficulty was that she had only two of the skill areas at a sufficiently high level. This presented problems not only because she could not manage the school in a comfortable way, but also because her own individual development as a human being was being frustrated. So, it is necessary for leadership to have the full range of skills.

Moreover, it is necessary for school districts to insist that leadership have all these skills, for only in this way will environments be reinforced that will help individuals grow rather than be locked into a static level of value development. Institutions need to encourage the kind of leadership that is integrated, holistic and ethical in its development.

In schools, one teacher may be very enthusiastic about behavior modification as a means of aiding students. Another may be devoted to cognitive development, trying to convey a great deal of information to the child. In the latter case, the Instrumental skills receive nearly exclusive attention, a tendency that has constituted the main thrust of traditional education. There has been little effort, for example, to acquaint teachers with the kinds of skills they might gainfully use in dealing with the educational system itself.

An awareness of the four skill areas and of their relationship to values can help teachers to see things more holistically. They have all the skills we need in the present world. All the values that we speak of are operative. These simply need to be brought into harmony and integrated into individual persons and into the institutions of our society.

VALUES IN EDUCATION

In the last three sections we have examined the nature of value patterns that can both reveal the degree of human maturation and suggest a path for future growth in individuals and institutions. In this section, we shall offer some ideas about how the principles of value development can be applied to the nation's formal educational systems. We want to suggest not only ways to improve the institutional performance of the schools, but also ways by which values-based education can modify the curriculum in order to insure the steady growth of students toward the full realization of their humanity.

Critical to the achievement of educational objectives is a smoothly running school in which leadership on the part of both administrators and teachers is functioning at the highest possible level of consciousness. It is also important to realize that leadership styles can be appropriate or inappropriate for the tasks of the school. It is up to those charged with directing the school system to be aware of the style necessary for congruence with the institution's mission.

Phases and Educational Leadership

Phase I Leadership operating at this Phase is DICTATORIAL, with an emphasis on Autocratic decision making. The superintendent, principal or teacher will:

- Maintain physical and social distance from followers
- Make all major decisions
- Seek to control as much as possible
- Demand loyalty to her/him as well as to the school

Followership at this Phase is characterized by:

- Viewing the leader as distant and unapproachable
- Docility, blind obedience, passivity
- Seeing the leader as having an aura of infallibility around her or him
- Infantile type behavior

While such a style may be necessary in times of imminent danger, it becomes destructive of other educational goals when the environment is secure. It is unlikely that such a leader will be able to delegate any activities which may seem to diminish her or his power or will listen to input from teachers and staff persons in the schools. It is particularly stressful when the followership is valuing on a more advanced level and experiences the leader's style as oppressive and unjust.

Phase I Growing to Phase II   Leadership in this Phase is BENEVOLENT, exercising Parental authority. The administrator or teacher will:

* Listen to subordinates but reserve decision making to herself or himself
* Demand loyalty to superiors and insure the careful following of the rules

Followership at this Phase is characterized by:

* Feeling cared for as a child would
* Dependency
* Viewing the leader as approachable, but recognizing that she or he has the last word

Leadership operating out of this Phase is appropriate when the leader is highly skilled and the followers are not. Relationships are based on fairness and mutual respect. Laws and rules are expected to be followed so as to maintain an ordered environment. The style becomes dysfunctional when excessive rigidity and perfectionism are apparent and when followers demand more autonomy and individual responsibility. For teachers in the primary grades, such a leadership style with respect to students may be appropriate, but only if such a stance is taken consciously and with openness to opportunities for growth.

Phase II   Leadership in this Phase is MANAGERIAL, with an emphasis on Bureaucratic efficiency. The administrator or teacher will:

* Manage by objectives, stressing order, clear policies, goals and rules
* Demand respect and loyalty to institutions, their goals and systems
* Delegate only to those who are skilled and loyal to the institution

Followership in this Phase is characterized by:

* Viewing the leader as approachable and a good listener
* Seeing tasks and expectations as clear
* Accepting the exercise of delegated authority in defined areas

For the education leader, the skills most needed at this level are interpersonal and social ones as well as skills in one's discipline. As in the previous Phase, there is also the danger of rigidity and resistance to change. On a personal level, the leader may also feel the tension between loyalty to the institution and the need to spend time with family.

Phase II Growing to Phase III   Leadership in this Phase is FACILITATIVE, with an emphasis on Empowerment. It is a transitional style in which one is moving from the previous Phases which stress efficiency, hierarchical chains of command and control to more democratic, participatory and collaborative styles of leadership. Leaders will:

- Be caught between efficiency and human needs, trying to find a balance between institutional demands and personal values
- Be uncertain in making decisions
- Act as listener, clarifier

Followership will be characterized by:

- Willingness to express feelings
- Confusion due to mixed signals from leader
- The need for good interpersonal skills

The leader in this Phase is less certain than before about her or his beliefs and feelings. A search for new meaning and values leads one to look for a personal path that may lead away from loyalty to the institution and its stated mission. She or he may struggle between meeting the needs of the institution and being sensitive to the more personal needs of her or his employees or students. It is a time of confusion and searching for the balance between these often opposing factors; hence, it may also be a time of inaction, because it is simply too difficult to make decisions. It is crucial for persons operating at this Phase to learn the Interpersonal, Imaginal and Systems skills that will enable them to make wise decisions which meet both institutional needs and those of the individuals in the institution, or they face the risk of returning to a more bureaucratic and controlling management or leadership style.

Phase III   Leadership in this Phase is COLLABORATIVE, with an emphasis on Democratic participation. Leaders will:

- Be democratic in their style
- Have clear vision about how to make institutions more human
- Be able to modify rules according to personal conscience

Followership will be characterized by:

- Small group interactions
- Participation as peers in some decision making
- Having the need to develop group dynamics skills, including those of conflict resolution

This is the ideal level for school leadership, particularly at the secondary level and in higher education. Individuals have passed successfully through the often paralyzing laissez-faire period and now have a new sense of personal creative energy and a renewed vision of an institution that can be efficient, as well as dignifying, for its members. Given the high level of interaction at which individuals are now functioning, issues of time management become critical. It becomes imperative that each has support structures, such as a group of respected peers and trusted friends, as well as people of the same professional status and ability with whom ideas and problems can be shared regularly. Because leaders of this type are in high demand, issues of time management, stress and personal health are more important than ever. The individual is in danger, moreover, of becoming too independent and over-committed. Values of leisure and contemplation become important.

Phase III Growing to IV   Leadership in this Phase is in the role of SERVANT. The leader will:

- Be concerned with the quality of interaction in the organization and its impact on society as well as with productivity
- Seek to maximize development of individuals within the system
- Foster interdependent governance by peer teams on the basis of agreed upon values
- Encourage group decision making as a normal process along with mutual responsibility and collegiality

Followership will be characterized by:

- Willingness to take responsibility
- Ability to live and work at high levels of trust and intimacy
- Well-developed Imaginal skills

At this level of leadership, the administrator has an acute awareness of the rights of all human beings, not just those in her or his organization. Within the organization, decisions are made collaboratively, and authority is always shared cooperatively. Persons operating at this advanced level must learn new skills—the most critical being the skills that will help them to balance their involvement in the development of just and humane institutions with ample time for solitude and intimacy.

Phase IV   Leadership in this Phase represents the highest level of conscious-ness and is found only rarely. At this point, leadership and followership are merged, the concepts becoming meaningless. All activity is interdependent in nature and global in concern. At this level, the prophet educator is dedicated to calling us to improve the balance between the world of material goods and the needs of each human being; to work on issues related to ecology, human rights, reconciliation of conflicting groups and the creative and humane use of technology.

It is well to remember that leadership style generates, and often is supported by, a corresponding followership style. A leader who is autocratic will encourage followership that is consistently docile and obedient. If the mission is to defend the school against physical threats from hostile elements in the community, then a battlefield leadership style is perhaps appropriate. If the external threat is more fancied than real, such a leadership style will not only be inappropriate but will also provide an institutional environment that will make development toward higher levels of maturity more difficult.

Information gained from examining Phases of Consciousness can be a key factor in understanding student and teacher needs, leadership styles, individual ethical orientations, and other personal and institutional aspects. But important to remember are the skills that lie behind the values being developed. For example, the value of Self-Worth requires verbal, cognitive and interpersonal skills in order to share information and ideas. If one does not learn these skills, then she or he can never be valued or esteemed for her or his uniqueness as a person.

Values-Based Education

No education is neutral. Any curriculum, teaching method, or code of rules will be reinforcing some values and weakening others. The choice for the educator is not between neutrality and some set of values, but between implicit and explicit values. It is better to make the values within the educational unit explicit, thus making it possible both to assess a set of values for coherence and to adapt value development strategies to the level appropriate for the student's stage of development.

Never before in human history has the need been greater for clear thinking about values and value differences. Technological development has brought us face-to-face with many complex issues involving difficult value choices at both the individual and the organizational level.

Our children and young people are the future leaders of our societies, yet our schools are faced with growing numbers of students who are not experiencing success. The characteristics of these students are well known:

* Lack of self-worth
* Seeing themselves as dumb rather than unskilled
* Avoidance behavior

- Distrust of adults and adult institutions
- Limited and often negative notions of the future
- Inadequate peer relationships
- Impatience
- Disruptive tendencies
- Inability to see a relationship between effort and achievement

It is therefore essential that values education be at the heart of the learning process in elementary, secondary and adult education.

The importance of values and values education is as old as civilization itself. Socrates talked about the meaning of justice and truth. Aristotle was concerned about the hierarchy of virtues and what was needed for the good life. Today, we speak of the value priorities that each person needs in order to be a productive and creative member of society. What has been understood for centuries through western religious and philosophic traditions is that values motivate the individual person and guide moral and ethical behavior.

Developing a Values-Based Curriculum

Teachers can intentionally focus on particular values and their appropriate skills when they recognize that these are an integral part of a curriculum in any given subject. Therefore, values can be taught in the regular curriculum by using values based educational techniques. Every curriculum has values, and many teachers are unconsciously teaching them. One only need analyze the value-laden words contained in educational objectives to quickly identify which values are implicitly being taught in that curriculum.

Unfortunately, by taking the approach of not consciously developing a value-related curriculum, the educational program tends to drive the values. It is the educators, of course, who should decide when values are to be embodied by the program. If not, the values tend to be introduced at random at inappropriate levels of student consciousness and are not understood, let alone assimilated.

Teachers first should agree on a list of values to be included in the curriculum and then decide at what grade levels they should be introduced. They would then formulate specific learning objectives which would emerge from a careful consideration of the meaning of each of the values and, using the skills related to the values, design appropriate teaching strategies. For example, suppose that curriculum planners decided that one learning outcome of the K–12 program should be that "Students will be willing to support efforts to insure a safe and reliable food supply for all the world's peoples." Values based educators would examine plans for the early grades and modify them to include skills in growing and caring for food plants, building a compost pile, or other specific projects which would constitute first steps in the development of an ecological vision at a global level. Subsequent activities might include science fair entries, field trips to nearby farms, studies of the effects of chemicals on soils, and the like.

By the time students reached high school biology courses, the ground would have been laid for fruitful investigation of the interconnectedness between scientific knowledge and the value issues related to the equitable distribution of the world's nutritional resources. In social studies, students would also learn about how development strategies in Third World nations can be improved so that those nations are able to grow their own food and preserve the quality of the food produced. The point is that students should be introduced to values and skills appropriate to their age group and their level of consciousness. The curriculum should insure a path to more fully developed value clusters as students advance through the grades.

Planning for Curriculum Change

While every school system might not agree with the choice of the above curriculum design, it is important that as many people as possible within the community and the schools meet to decide what those values will be. From there, the system can begin to fashion an effective values based curriculum. The following procedural steps can be a model for determining values:

1. Develop a working committee with wide representation across a school system and among community groups.
2. Develop a list of core values which the curriculum will help students internalize. Such a list might include:
    * Responsibility
    * Service/Vocation
    * Competence/Confidence
    * Independence
3. Reach a consensus among teachers, administrators, parents, board members and members of the community on the specific meaning of each value.
4. Develop committees of teachers, parents and students to help all students develop Individual Learning Plans.
5. Identify the values and skills which need to be addressed in the various

age levels to enable students to achieve objectives by the end of their senior year.

6. Prepare evaluation procedures to monitor the students' progress as they move through the program.

7. Adjust the curriculum and specific plans as needed in light of the evaluations.

It is important to realize that preparing specific learning plans requires the incorporation of affective objectives to supplement cognitive and psychomotor ones. If the curriculum calls for increasing the self-esteem of students, then it is important that class activities be organized so that each student can feel a sense of Self-Worth. Self-Worth, of course, is enhanced when students can demonstrate Competence.

It is particularly important for students in grades K–8 to acquire Instrumental and Interpersonal skills appropriate to value development in Phases I and II. As students develop basic skills in reading, communication and calculating, they also develop Self-Confidence and Self-Esteem. Moreover, if the Instrumental skills are taught with an added emphasis on affirmation of Self-Esteem, they will be learned more easily and effectively. The affective and the cognitive/psychomotor then become mutually reinforcing. Similarly, the ability to relate to others positively by using such interpersonal skills as sharing, empathy, compromise and speaking appropriately can enhance achievement in academic areas. The teacher can encourage collaborative learning activities in which each person has an important part to play in completing assignments, solving problems and in making presentations. Teachers can guard against students who exclude others, who engage in name calling or other "put down" behavior. They can also make sure that students compliment each other or support one another in other ways.

Each lesson plan, therefore, should include not only objectives in the affective area, but also include a specifically designed set of strategies and evaluation procedures which will insure that the appropriate values are systematically attained.

Conclusion

Education for excellence in any culture is always going to be concerned about the values and moral integrity of students. Education needs to contain within its objectives not only the nurturing of knowledge, but also the development of virtuous leaders. If we are to deal successfully with the increasing complexity of our institutions and respond to the need for a new type of relationship among the individuals who work in them, we cannot be satisfied with simply teaching the technologies of the new "information super-highway." More than ever before, individuals need clear priorities to cope with the flood of information, and these priorities must be grounded in human and humane values.

Moreover, increased corporate complexity is simply a sign of a more complex world that calls for the best use of the resources we have in order to not only build more human institutions but also encourage the development of sound ethical leadership needed to manage them. This does not mean a loss of efficiency and productivity. It means the expansion of efficiency and productivity through collaborative systems which improve the corporate environment and can have a positive influence on the larger community as well.

Educators, whether they be teachers, parents or administrators, all with different tasks, responsibilities and needs, can find themselves a part of a more cohesive school system when the basic ingredients that drive the system and give it purpose are identified. Those schools that are clear about their values are the ones most likely to be effective in the long term if they integrate those values into all aspects of the school system: behavioral norms, philosophical statements, hiring practices, educational and inservice programs and management structures.

It is these schools that can have the most positive moral effect on our own society and can contribute in some manner to a better global society where peace, learning and respect for differences become the norm rather than war, mistrust and oppression. When this happens, the quality of the learning environment is enhanced and the educational climate becomes conducive to higher levels of creativity and participation.

Skills for Teachers

Skills for Teachers

A S WE HAVE seen in Section I, important life skills fall into four categories related to our abilities to do things, to relate to other people, to use our imagination and to master systems. When we look at these four kinds of skills, we can make a useful connection between these four categories, the values, the Four Phases of Consciousness and the other developmental factors that can cause a shift in personal consciousness (*Values Shift*, p. 100) The figure below shows the relationship of the development of these four skill types to the Four Phases of Consciousness:

Skill Development and the Four Phases of Consciousness

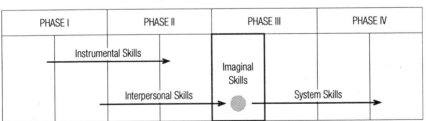

Fig. 3

In the process of value development, teachers can use the *Teacher's Journal* (see Section III) to analyze their own behavior, identify the values implicit in their daily activities and choices, and to classify these values as Foundation, Focus, or Future (see pg. 33). To fully internalize Focus or Future values, it is necessary to identify the related skills and begin to practice them preferably with the guidance of a competent coach. For each of the skill areas, this section includes a series of exercises designed to help teachers acquire the various skills.

EXERCISES FOR TEACHERS TO DEVELOP INSTRUMENTAL SKILLS

Instrumental Skills: the abilities that enable teachers to get a job done; the intellectual and physical competencies that enable them to shape both ideas and the learning environment; the skills involved in cognitive accomplishments. Instrumental skills combine tools and the intellect—a combination required in any profession.

Examples of Instrumental Skills for Teachers
1. Writing and implementing successful lesson plans.
2. Speaking effectively with students about thoughts and feelings.
3. Listening attentively and paraphrasing accurately.
4. Expressing thoughts and feelings in writing.
5. Using a large and discriminating vocabulary.
6. Reading quickly, and with comprehension, educational research.

Instrumental skills are task-oriented. They include those general skills taught by Elementary Teachers necessary for literacy: reading, writing, speaking, handling numbers and operating computers. For teachers they include all the specialized skills of the teaching profession.

Since most of formal teacher education is concerned with developing instrumental skills, this section is brief and concentrates on a few skills that are often overlooked.

Identifying Instrumental Skills

1. Understanding and Prioritizing Instrumental Skills
Objectives: (1) Teachers will be able to illustrate the concept of Instrumental skills through examples. (2) Teachers will be able to reflect on the importance of such skills.

* Explain the concept of Instrumental skills to your teaching staff.
* Make a list of Instrumental skills for teachers, taking into account

your mission statement, organizational goals and educational philosophy.

* Ask each teacher to mark the list as follows:
  * "M" for the skills you feel are of most importance for a teacher to be successful.
  * "O" for those you feel are often important for a teacher to be successful.
  * "S" for those that are somewhat important for a teacher to be successful.
  * "N" for those that are not important for a teacher to be successful.

	SKILL	MARK
1.		
2.		
3.		
4.		
5.		
6.		
7.		
8.		
9.		
10.		

* Describe a learning strategy for each skill marked "M" or "O."

2. Tools for Teaching

A tool is any instrument that is used to accomplish a task in such a way that the user controls the form and quality of the product. Instrumental skills can be viewed as the skills of using tools. At a somewhat more sophisticated level, they include the skills of designing and making tools. It is important to understand that tool-making is a highly professional activity. Teachers who are fully involved in their work usually invent shortcuts, tricks of the trade, handy helps. Many publications for teachers are full of such helpful hints which are expressions of human creativity. Therefore, another way of analyzing Instrumental skills is to look at the tools being used —especially those teachers have made for themselves.

Objectives: (1) Teachers will be able to expand the analysis of their Instrumental skills. (2) Teachers will improve their self-image as competent persons.

  * Ask the teachers to form cooperative groups and list the teaching tools they have used in the last month. Then have them respond to the following questions.
     * *Which do you use most often?*
     * *Which would you not have used three years ago?*
     * *Which are you able to repair?*
     * *Have you ever made any tools?*
     * *Have you ever improvised a tool or made do with whatever materials and equipment happened to be on hand?*

Devleoping Decision Making Skills

1. Clarifying Values and Objectives

Teachers make numerous decisions every day of their lives, from what to put on in the morning to which course or job to take or which friendship to develop. Teachers vary greatly in their approaches to decision-making; some are quick and confident, others need time; some never look back, others anguish over a decision even after it is made, wondering whether they have "done the right thing." Some may be paralyzed, particularly before an important decision, hoping that circumstances will decide the matter for them or perhaps half expecting to find an answer from heaven under the pillow when they awake in the morning. These differences are partly a matter of temperament, partly a matter of training. Often it is overlooked that decision-making is an area for training. In fact, there are skills involved in deciding—skills that can be learned, that can help to reduce anxieties and improve decision-making.

A good decision is not necessarily one that turns out well; rather it is one that is made well. Among the steps that enter into a well-made decision are: clarifying values and goals, developing alternative courses of action, gathering and assessing relevant information and assessing the consequences of the various alternatives. The process does not follow a smooth course. Seeking information about alternatives often leads to the development of new alternatives, which in turn may result in a reassessment of priorities. When the decision is an important one, such as the choice of a college major, a career, a place to live, or a life partner, individuals may shift back and forth between the various steps several times before gaining sufficient clarity to move into action. When teachers feel uncertain or even paralyzed in the face of big decisions, a conscious, systematic approach can be particularly useful. The following exercises can help develop some of the Instrumental skills that enter into informed decision making.

Objectives: (1) Teachers will be able to analyze the values operating in an important decision. (2) Teachers will be able to identify the possible outcomes in a difficult emotional situation. (3) Teachers will be able to relate the values to objectives or outcomes.

* Read the following to the teachers:

> John is a second grade teacher in a small southern town. He is very concerned about a student in his class named Dan. Dan has been falling asleep in class and is very aggressive toward other students. Recently, he tried to cut another student's hair; then, stabbed himself on the hand with the scissors. John is concerned that if he tells Dan's parents Dan will be beaten, as Dan has described beatings to him in the past resulting from bad reports at school. He has reported the situation to the authorities who indicate they can do nothing without hard evidence. The school has scheduled psychological testing for Dan, but the wait is nine weeks for testing and several months for placement. John feels torn about what to do.

* Have the teachers form cooperative groups and list five of John's possible objectives (i.e., the outcomes he desires).

1.

2.

3.

4.

5.

* Now have them list five values they can identify in John's case. Are any of the values in conflict? *(See Value Definitions, pp. 151 ff.)*

1.

2.

3.

4.

5.

* Ask the groups to prioritize the values according to their own views.

1.

2.

3.

4.

5.

* Have the groups discuss the following questions: *Could you prioritize the values differently? If so, would your choice of an objective for John be different?*

2. Developing and Assessing Alternatives

Unless a teacher has at least two alternatives, there is no need to make a decision; but often there are many more alternatives in a given situation.

Objectives: (1) Teachers will be able to develop alternatives for a given situation. (2) Teachers will be able to assess the advantages and disadvantages of each alternative.

- Have teachers form cooperative groups, then ask the teachers to brainstorm alternatives for John. Ask them to let their imaginations flow freely. Ask that they think the unthinkable, to let unpleasant as well as pleasant alternatives rise to the surface.
- Have them assess the advantages of each alternative, using the following chart:

ALTERNATIVE #1   PROBABLE OUTCOME

                                        1.

                                        2.

                                        3.

                                        4.

ALTERNATIVE #2   PROBABLE OUTCOME

                                        1.

                                        2.

                                        3.

                                        4.

ALTERNATIVE #3   PROBABLE OUTCOME

                                        1.

                                        2.

                                        3.

                                        4.

3. Evaluating Information

Gathering and evaluating information is an important part of decision-making. Reliable information can open up new alternatives and enable teachers to predict the outcome of a given course of action with accuracy.

Objectives: (1) Teachers will be able to identify sources of information. (2) Teachers will be able to evaluate sources of information.

* Read the following to the teachers:

> Pamela is beginning a Master's program which could lead to certification as a school administrator. She is thinking about entering the certification program and moving towards a career change, but feels bewildered and uncertain about where to turn. She very much loves teaching, but feels she can have more impact as an administrator.

* Have the teachers form cooperative groups.
* Now ask them to imagine they are Pamela. See if any of the teachers have a different approach. If so, how does it differ from Pamela's. Ask the groups how Pamela can find the answers to these questions: *What does Pamela need to know? Here are three important sets of questions Pamela needs to ask herself:*
  1. What am I good at? What are my present skills and aptitudes?
  2. What do I enjoy doing? What are my interests? My likes and dislikes?
  3. What are the career possibilities in the fields of my interest?
* Have the groups compare their answers with these: *How can Pamela determine whether to enter the administration program?*
  1. By examining personal history such as teaching experience, leadership roles, volunteer activities.
  2. By discussing the program in depth with a university advisor.
  3. By inviting feedback from her spouse, friends, fellow teachers and employers.

  How can Pamela assess her interests?
  1. By keeping a diary and then looking at her best days, she will get one indicator of activities she particularly enjoys.
  2. By evaluating the use of her free time in the past month.
  3. By dreaming about what she would do if time and money were no obstacle.

4. By taking vocational and interest tests at a guidance center.
How can Pamela find out about possibilities in administration?
1. By talking to Administrators.
2. By getting an internship or a summer job in administration.
3. By reading biographies of practitioners.
4. By scanning journals or newsletters for people in the field.

4. Approaches to Risk Taking

How much information is enough? There is no absolute answer to this question. At some point, the search for additional information becomes an evasion of the decision, and we are faced with the paradox that "not to decide is to decide." Every decision entails some risks, for we never can have all the relevant information nor can we predict accurately all outcomes. Hence, the need arises for risk-taking strategies which weigh the probabilities and desirability of various outcomes against each other.

Objective: Teachers will be able to identify various risk-taking strategies.
* Place a waste basket in front of the room and mark three lines on the floor. Line A should be five feet away from the basket; line B, ten feet away; line C, 20 feet away. Ask your teachers to form cooperative groups.
* Each member of the group chooses the line on which to stand, and takes three turns at tossing a piece of crumpled paper into the basket.
* Participants are scored as follows:

1 point for each basket from line A (5' from basket)   _____
2 points for each basket from line B (10' from basket)   _____
4 points for each basket from line C (20' from basket)   _____ .
                                            TOTAL SCORE   _____

The person with the highest score receives a prize.

The two factors involved are the amount of risk and the desirability of the outcome. We can describe the three most common strategies as follows:

High risk/high desirability: the long shot, the wishful thinker, the gambler who is ready "to go for broke" on a slim chance.

Low risk/low desirability: the safe shot, for the person who wants to be sure of getting something, or, at least, of avoiding the worst. "The ship in the harbor is safe, but that's not what ships are for."

Low to medium risk/high desirability: a realistic strategy that tries for the best combination of desirability and probability of success.

There is a fourth possibility: *High risk/low desirability.* At first glance, it seems unlikely that anyone would choose this strategy, but perhaps it describes the person who keeps on "hitting her or his head against a stone wall," the one who stays in an unsuitable career, risking health and psychological well-being rather than changing to something more desirable; the battered wife who remains in the marriage; the self-punishing drug addict.

EXERCISES FOR TEACHERS TO DEVELOP INTERPERSONAL SKILLS

Interpersonal Skills: the ability to facilitate communication, mutual understanding and cooperation. Our interpersonal skill potential grows out of our family relationships and our early social experiences.

Examples of Interpersonal Skills

1   Identifying a student's feelings accurately.
2. Expressing feelings openly.
3. Accepting personal worth, and feeling good about oneself.
4. Being aware of expectations of oneself.
5. Accepting limitations peacefully.
6. Identifying negative feelings and expressing them appropriately.
7. Accepting positive feedback non-apologetically.
8. Accepting negative feedback non-defensively.
9. Reading non-verbal communication accurately.
10. Expressing goals and intentions clearly.
11. Dealing effectively with mixed messages.
12. Remaining calm in a highly stressful situation.
13. Giving positive feedback so that students feel affirmed.
14. Giving negative feedback appropriately.
15. Expressing feelings non-verbally and symbolically.
16. Describing student behavior non-judgmentally.
17. Accepting students and families whose values are very unlike one's own.
18. Showing appreciation for the strengths of others, enjoying others.
19. Checking perceptions of students' ideas, feelings or values with them.
20. Taking responsibility for meeting one's own needs rather than expecting others to meet them.
21. Negotiating needs and wants in a relationship.
22. Distinguishing feelings from opinions.
23. Expressing one's own values without judging different values held by others.
24. Being open to new values, attitudes, experiences.

Teachers are social beings. They depend on each other for the full development of potentialities. Even creative geniuses in the arts or sciences cannot bring forth the new without interaction with others in their field. A Mozart is only possible where a musical family and culture are prepared to nourish so extraordinary a talent. Most of us only grow into responsible, caring human beings in a supportive network of human relationships.

Interpersonal skills, then, are the skills necessary to develop satisfying human relationships. They enable teachers to perceive themselves and others accurately and sympathetically. They facilitate communication, mutual understanding and cooperation.

Developing Self-Awareness

Clear communication depends upon teachers being in touch with themselves. This includes their body, feelings, thoughts, intentions and actions. At any moment, a great deal is going on in and around teachers. Usually, they are aware of only a small fraction of the wealth of information available about themselves. No one can be totally self-aware all the time, but practicing brief periods of concentrated self-awareness can increase self-knowledge and enable teachers to make better choices about what they want to become and about what they want to share with others about themselves.

1. Tuning Into the Self

Adapted from John O. Stevens, *Awareness, Exploring, Experimenting Experiencing.*

Objectives: (1)Teachers will be better able to concentrate on the "here and now." (2) Teachers will be able to become more aware of their own body messages, feelings and thoughts.

- Find a place where your teachers can be comfortable, maybe sitting down or stretched out on the floor. Have them close their eyes, take a few deep breaths and exhale slowly.

- Have them pay attention to their own awareness. Ask them to say to themselves, "Now I am aware of ..." Tell them to try to focus their awareness on this instant and notice where the awareness goes. Ask if it is going to something inside the body or to something outside it.

- Have them focus outside their bodies. Ask what their senses are telling them about the here and now. What do they hear? smell? taste? Have them open their eyes—what do they see? Are they aware of the points where their body is touching the chair or the floor?

- Have them focus on their bodies and think about which parts come immediately into awareness and which parts do not give a clear sensation even when they focus on them.

* Now ask them to notice any feelings. A good place to begin is with the physical sensations in the body that usually accompany feelings, e.g., sweating, dry mouth, tense muscles, smiling, butterflies in the stomach, rapid heartbeat, etc. Ask if they are feeling excited, anxious, bored or whatever.
* Now have them pay attention to thoughts—the stream of ideas, beliefs, memories, plans, assumptions, evaluations, interpretations that pass through the mind.
* Have the teachers form small groups and discuss the following questions: *How did you feel during this exercise? What discoveries did you make about yourself?*

2. Using the Awareness Wheel

Adapted from Miller, Nunnally & Wackman, *Alive and Aware.*

Objectives: (1) Teachers will be able to increase their awareness of the amount of data available to them about themselves at any given moment. (2) Teachers will be able to distinguish clearly among sensory impressions, thoughts, feelings, intentions and actions.

Below is an explanation of the "Awareness Wheel," pictured on the next page.

The Awareness Wheel is a helpful device for bringing more of moment-to-moment experience into full awareness. Practicing with the Awareness Wheel can be an important step for teachers to learn to send clear messages.

Often teachers may have conflicting intentions or mixed feelings; in that case, tapping into the Awareness Wheel can be both a clarifying and a freeing experience.

"I see" refers to direct sensory experience, the immediate data supplied by eyes, ears, nose, taste, touch.

"I think" expresses an opinion, idea, belief, assumption, interpretation, evaluation, expectation or conclusion. "I see that you are frowning and I think I've done something to offend you." Actually, you have a headache. It is important to keep in mind that alternative interpretations are always possible, and that two people often come to very different interpretations of the same sensory data.

"I feel" refers to being pleased, uncomfortable, irritated, elated, bored, or whatever. Note that feelings can always be expressed by "I feel" followed by an adjective.

"I want" states a goal, aim or intention, i.e., what I want for myself in this situation. Often teachers fail to make intentions clear because they are unaware of them, or they think they are either obvious or unimportant, or they want to keep them hidden (e.g., "I want you to admire me"). Sometimes, intentions get expressed indirectly as "should," e.g., "You should finish that job" instead of "I would like you to ...."

"I act" names behavior. I may think I know what I am doing, but actually I am usually aware of only part of my behavior. My facial expressions, posture, tone of voice, and habitual gestures may be outside the focus of my attention and may be sending strong messages that interfere with my verbal communications.

- ❧ Have each teacher spend five minutes reflecting on the Awareness Wheel. Then have them write down their impressions.

- ❧ Ask the teachers to form small groups and discuss the following questions: *What came to you first? Most of us are more in touch with some parts of the wheel than with others. If you know this about yourself, can you increase your self-awareness by conscious attention to the other parts of the wheel? What difficulties did you experience in using the wheel? What did you discover about yourself?*

- ❧ In the fifteen statements below, one of the five dimensions of the Awareness Wheel is represented. Next to each statement, have the teachers indicate the dimension, using the following letters: *s* – sensing, *t* – thinking, *f* – feeling, *w* – wanting, *a* – acting.

1. *You don't even care how I feel about it.*
2. *I'm depressed because I didn't get the job.*
3. *My boss is a real jerk.*
4. *I see that you are upset.*
5. *I really don't feel like going to the dance tonight.*
6. *I'm so excited—John just called me!*
7. *I'm listening.*

8. *I'll take care of it first thing tomorrow.*
9. *Last night at dinner, I heard you say you wanted to see that show.*
10. *I stopped at the bank on the way home today.*
11. *I smell something good on the stove.*
12. *I'm a failure—I'll never amount to anything.*
13. *I'm really afraid to try.*
14. *I'd like to tell you how I'm feeling about our relationship.*
15. *I felt a cool breeze on my face.*

Answers: 1-t; 2-f; 3-t, (My opinion, or evaluation, probably with anger or resentment behind it); 4-t (My interpretation, I see tears, hear a shaky voice, see trembling hands, and infer "upset"); 5-w (Not a feeling but a desire, I want not to go); 6-f; 7-a (I am actively listening to you); 8-w (my intention); 9-s; 10-a; ll-s; 12-t (My opinion or conclusion, which may or may not be based on solid evidence); 13-F; 14-w; 15-s.

3. Automatic Writing

Objectives: (1) Teachers will be able to increase self-awareness and personal insight. (2) Teachers will be able to use free association as a means of getting in touch with concerns that are below their conscious awareness.

- Choose a stimulus phrase from the following list and ask each teacher to write for five minutes, without lifting pen from paper. Have each teacher write down whatever comes to mind, regardless of whether it relates to the stimulus phrase, and without worrying about grammar or spelling. Generally, the more quickly the words are written, the better. Either set an alarm clock to ring at the end of the pre-arranged time or appoint a timekeeper.

  Why am I in teaching?
  Who really knows me as a professional?
  I am presently aware that …
  When I think about my future, I feel …
  My greatest fear is …
  I am happiest when …
  My strongest point is …

- Have the teachers reflect on what they have written. Ask if they were aware of an "internal censor" in themselves that might have worried about sharing or even writing down some of these thoughts. Describe some of your concerns about taking risks.

- Ask teachers to form groups of two. Have each group discuss areas of common concern expressed in the writing.

- Have teachers discuss the role that the internal censor played and how it affected the writing.

4. Integrated Thinking: Getting in Touch With the Other Half of Your Brain
In recent years, science has become aware that each of us has not one, but two brains, the left hemisphere and the right. For right-handed people, the left hemisphere is dominant and contains speech, ideas, facts, concepts and thinking. The right hemisphere contains the symbolic, the intuitive, the imaginative and emotive (feelings). Because feelings are often in the non-cognitive hemisphere, it is often difficult to get in touch with them. This exercise may enable teachers to become more aware of the non-dominant hemisphere by allowing it to express itself through the non-dominant hand, "the hand not used to write with."

Objective: Teachers will become more aware of the non-dominant hemisphere of the brain.

- Have each teacher draw a picture of her/himself with the hand normally used to write with. The picture should include the whole body and contain as much detail as possible in five (5) minutes. Label this "Picture A."
- Ask them to set the picture aside and draw the same picture with their other hand. This picture should also include the whole body and contain as much detail as possible in five (5) minutes. Label this "Picture B."
- Have the teachers form groups of two and compare the two pictures. Using the following list of impressions ask them to write down each impression on the pictures which it best fits. Ask them to come to agreement on each picture if possible. Which picture looks:
  more youthful
  more relaxed
  more alive
  more happy
  more compassionate
  more loving
  more confident
  more attractive
  more open
  more alert

more intelligent
more energetic
more competent

- ❧ Have each teacher reflect on the words written on each of their pictures.
- ❧ Read the following to the teachers: *Picture "A" indicates how you see yourself and how you try to present yourself to others. Picture "B" may indicate how you really feel about yourself.*
- ❧ Ask them to discuss in which picture do they like themselves better? Why?

5. Becoming Aware of Your Self-Talk

Most of us carry on an internal dialogue with ourselves most of the time. This "self-talk" is usually sending us messages at a subliminal level, messages which may be either congratulatory or condemnatory: "I handled that pretty well." "I look terrible." Turning the full light of consciousness on teachers' self-talk enables them to test assumptions against reality. It is particularly useful for teachers to do this when dealing with negative feelings about themselves.

Objective: Teachers will become aware of self-talk and evaluate its underlying assumptions.

- ❧ Have teachers sit in a place in the room where they are comfortable, and can turn their attention inward. Ask them to think of a specific time when they felt sad, disappointed or depressed. Have them identify the reason for their feelings.
- ❧ Have them reflect on the following questions in writing to help them imagine, as concretely as possible, the specific situation:
  Where was I?
  What did the place look like?
  When was it?
  What time of day?
  What was I wearing?
  Who was there?
  With whom was I interacting?
  What is our relationship?
  What did I say/do?
  What did the other say/do?

How did I feel?

What was I saying to myself?

Was I saying any of the following?

> *I'm dumb.*
>
> *It was all my fault.*
>
> *... doesn't like me.*
>
> *I fouled up.*
>
> *I'll never be able to do ...*
>
> *It'll be a disaster if ... happens.*

✱ Ask them to review what they have written. Ask the teachers whether they are assuming any of the following?

I should be thoroughly competent and achieving in all respects.

Everyone I meet should like me.

It's terrible if things don't go the way I'd like.

Unhappiness is externally caused, and I cannot do anything about it.

My feelings are too strong to be controlled.

I have a right to be dependent; there should be somebody strong enough to take care of me.

My early childhood experiences determine my feelings and behavior — so I can't change.

It's easier to avoid difficulties than to face them.

There is invariably one right solution in every situation, and it is terrible if it isn't found.

✱ Ask them if they agree with any assumptions stated above? Then have them discuss in small groups how they would like to change them?

✱ Have the teachers reformulate the assumptions they disagree with into statements they can make with conviction, e.g., *I do not have to be perfect. My early childhood experiences do not irrevocably determine my behavior; I can do something about changing my behavior.*

✱ Ask the teachers to write their reformulated assumptions. Have them formulate a plan for practicing these new statements. Practice can include:

Taking a few minutes at the beginning and end of the day to repeat the new statement to themselves.

Writing the statement on a card or slip of paper and putting it where it will be seen every day.

Keeping a personal journal for a few weeks in which they note efforts to change self-talk.

6. Distinguishing Between Thoughts and Feelings

Many teachers have too small a vocabulary of feeling words to do justice to the complexity and richness of their feelings. Moreover, many have the common American habit of saying "I feel" when they intend to express a thought or an opinion rather than a feeling.

Objectives: (1) Teachers will be able to heighten their awareness of the difference between thoughts and feelings. (2) Teachers will be able to increase their vocabulary of feeling words. (3) Teachers will be able to describe their own feelings in non-judgmental language.

- Have the teachers form small groups and read them the following fantasy. *Imagine the following fantasy situation as vividly and in as much detail as possible.*

> Imagine that you are on a picnic in the country and are caught in a thunderstorm. The sky darkens, the wind blows more strongly. You hear the rumbles of distant thunder and hastily start to gather up your belongings. The lightning flashes light up heavy masses of black clouds. Slowly the rain begins, until it becomes a steady downpour. Feel the raindrops hitting you. The lightning hits a tree near you, ripping off a limb. You can hardly manage to walk against the wind. You smell the air and the wet earth, as you struggle toward your car. Suddenly, the storm ends and the sun appears.

- After reading this fantasy pose the following to the teachers: *What are you aware of right now as the fantasy mood ends? Write down your responses. Does your answer tell you anything about yourself?*
- Invite the teachers to share their answers with the group.
- Ask each group to discuss the following: *Did people tend to answer more with feelings, thoughts, or descriptive statements? If you answered with thoughts or descriptions, what were your feelings?*
- Have the groups brainstorm and write down all the feeling words mentioned in the above discussion.
- Ask them to compare the list with the following list of Feeling Words from Rosenberg's list. (*See pg 76.*) The group may want to spend time discussing the shades of meaning conveyed by some of the words they do not ordinarily use.

Feeling Words (Marshall Rosenberg)

POSITIVE		NEGATIVE		
absorbed	helpful	afraid	disturbed	mad
adventurous	hopeful	aggravated	down	mean
affectionate	inquisitive	agitation	embittered	melancholy
alert	inspired	alarm	exasperated	miserable
alive	intense	aloof	exhausted	mope
amazed	interested	angry	fatigued	pessimistic
amused	intrigued	animosity	fearful	provoked
animated	invigorated	annoyance	fidgety	puzzled
appreciative	involved	anxious	flaky	rattled
astonished	joyful	apathetic	forlorn	reluctant
blissful	jubilant	apprehensive	frightened	repelled
breathless	keyed up	aversion	frustrated	resentful
buoyant	loving	bad	furious	restless
calm	mellow	beat	gloomy	sad
carefree	merry	bitter	grief	scared
cheerful	mirthful	blah	grumpy	sensitive
comfortable	moved	blown up	guilty	shaky
composed	optimistic	blue	hate	shocked
concerned	overwhelmed	bored	heavy	skeptical
confident	overjoyed	burned up	helpless	sleepy
contented	peaceful	breathless	hesitant	sorrowful
cool	pleasant	brokenhearted	horrified	sorry
curious	proud	chagrined	horrible	sour
dazzled	quiet	cold	hostile	spiritless
delighted	radiant	concerned	hot	startled
eager	refreshed	confused	humdrum	surprised
ecstatic	relieved	cool	hurt '	suspicion
elated	satisfied	cross	impatient	tepid
electrified	secure	credulous	indifferent	terrified
encouraged	sensitive	critical	inert	thwarted
engrossed	spellbound	dejected	infuriated	tired
enjoyment	splendid	depressed	insecure	troubled
enlivened	stimulated	despair	insensitive	uncomfortable
enthusiastic	surprised	despondent	intense	unconcerned
exalted	tender	detached	irate	uneasy
excited	tenderness	disappointed	irked	unglued
exhilarated	thankful	discouraged	irritated	unhappy
expansive	thrilled	disgruntled	jealous	unnerved
expectant	touched	disgusted	jittery	unsteady
exuberant	tranquil	disheartened	keyed-up	upset
fascinated	trusting	dislike	lassitude	uptight
free	warm	dismayed	lazy	weary
friendly	wide-awake	displeased	let down	withdrawn
fulfilled		disquieted	lethargic	woeful
good-humored		dissatisfied	listless	worried
grateful		distant	lonely	wretched
happy		distressed		

An Alternative Fantasy

Imagine that you are walking down a country road on a hot, sunny day. The road is dusty, and you breathe in some of the dust. You pass an abandoned house, the windows broken and the door hanging by one hinge. You come to a covered bridge. It is a long, dark tunnel—you cannot see the light at the other end. It smells damp and musty. A spider web brushes across your face. Your footsteps echo in the darkness. You can hear the water of the creek rushing beneath you. Suddenly you step on a rotten board and your foot goes through. You catch a glimpse of rocks and dark water beneath you. You grab a post and haul your foot back up, scratching your leg on the broken board. You begin to run, gasping for breath, hardly able to breathe the dead musty air. Finally, you see the light and stumble out onto a grassy bank in the sunshine.

7. Identifying Feelings

Objectives: (1) Teachers will be better able to distinguish clear from unclear expressions of feelings. (2) Teachers will be able to revise mixed or unclear statements in order to make clear statements of feelings.

- ❧ Ask the teachers to put a check mark next to each of the following statements which clearly expresses the speaker's feelings. Then try to rewrite the others.

1. *I feel you are the most selfish person I've ever met.*
2. *We all feel you're a wonderful person.*
3. *I feel put down.*
4. *I'm really angry that you were so late for dinner.*
5. *I feel we should focus on finding a way to fight the increase in nuclear power plants.*
6. *I feel misunderstood.*
7. *Can't you see I'm busy?*
8. *I feel that you are really inaccessible.*
9. *I feel that you're being unfair.*
10. *I felt upset when you interrupted my story at the dinner last night.*

- ❧ Explain that the words "I feel that" always introduce a thought or opinion. Feelings are facts and do not admit of argument. But opinions are interpretations; my interpretation can differ from yours, and there is room for argument. Introducing an opinion under the cover of "I feel" often effectively stifles disagreement, or at least makes free discussion more difficult.

✺   Explain that some feeling words contain overtones of blaming: "I feel put down or ripped off or ignored." Such words imply that the other is at fault, and will therefore provoke defensiveness. Try to express your own feelings without blaming anyone else.

8. Identifying Personality Types

There are many typologies available to teachers for understanding different types of personality. One useful typology is the Jungian classification of thinking/feeling, intuitive/sensate, extravert/introvert, structure/flow (or, in the terms used in the following inventory, judging/perceiving).

The following Personal Style Inventory will enable teachers to gain insight into themselves in light of these dimensions.

Objective: Teachers will gain self insight into dimensions of their personalities by using the Personal Style Inventory.

Personal Style Inventory

Just as every person has differently shaped feet and toes from every other person, so we all have differently "shaped" personalities. Just as no person's foot shape is "right" or "wrong," so no person's personality shape is right or wrong. The purpose of this inventory is to give teachers a picture of the shape of their preferences, but that shape, while different from the shapes of other persons' personalities, has nothing to do with mental health or mental problems.

✺   Provide teachers with the following instructions.

> The following items are arranged in pairs (A and B), and each member of the pair represents a preference you may or may not hold. Rate your preference for each item by giving it a score of 0 to 5 (0 meaning you really feel negative about it or strongly about the other member of the pair, 5 meaning you strongly prefer it or do not prefer the other member of the pair). The scores for *a* and *b* MUST ADD UP TO 5 (0 and 5, 1 and 4, 2 and 3, etc.). Do not use fractions such as 2½.

> © D. W. Champagne and R. C. Hogan. Reprinted and adapted with permission of the authors from the privately published book, *Supervisory and Management Skills: A Competency Based Training Program for Middle Managers of Educational Systems* by D. W. Champagne and R. C. Hogan.

I prefer:

1. a. ___ making decisions after finding out what other educators think
   b. ___ making decisions without consulting others
2. a. ___ being called imaginative or intuitive
   b. ___ being called factual and accurate
3. a. ___ making decisions about students based on available data and systematic analysis of situations
   b. ___ making decisions about students based on empathy, feelings, and understanding their needs and values
4. a. ___ allowing commitments to occur if others want to make them
   b. ___ pushing for definite commitments to ensure that they are made
5. a. ___ quiet, thoughtful time alone for planning
   b. ___ active, energetic planning time with other teachers
6. a. ___ using teaching methods that I know are effective
   b. ___ trying to think of new methods of teaching
7. a. ___ grading based on unemotional logic and careful set-by-step analysis
   b. ___ grading based on what I feel and believe about students from experience
8. a. ___ avoiding deadlines for student work
   b. ___ setting deadlines and sticking to them
9. a. ___ at meetings, thinking a lot before speaking
   b. ___ speaking freely for an extended period and thinking at a later time
10. a. ___ thinking about possibilities
    b. ___ dealing with actualities
11. a. ___ being thought of as a thinking person
    b. ___ being thought of as a feeling person
12. a. ___ considering every possible angle for a long time before and after making a decision
    b. ___ getting the information I need, considering it for a while, and then a fairly quick, firm decision
13. a. ___ inner thoughts and feelings others cannot see
    b. ___ activities and occurrences in which others join
14. a. ___ the abstract or theoretical
    b. ___ the concrete or real
15. a. ___ helping students explore their feelings
    b. ___ helping students make logical decisions
16. a. ___ change, and keeping options open
    b. ___ predictability, and knowing in advance
17. a. ___ communicating little of my inner thinking and feelings
    b. ___ communicating freely my inner thinking and feelings
18. a. ___ possible views of the whole
    b. ___ the factual details available
19. a. ___ using common sense and conviction to make decisions
    b. ___ using data, analysis, and reason to make decisions
20. a. ___ planning ahead based on projections

b. ___   planning as necessities arise, just before carrying out the plans

21.   a. ___   meeting new people
      b. ___   being alone or with one person I know well

22.   a. ___   ideas
      b. ___   facts

23.   a. ___   convictions
      b. ___   variable conclusions

24.   a. ___   keeping written lesson plans updated and in notebooks as much as possible
      b. ___   using written lesson plans as little as possible (although I may use them)

25.   a. ___   discussing a new, unconsidered issue at length with a team of teachers
      b. ___   puzzling out issues in my mind, then sharing the results with other teachers

26.   a. ___   carrying out carefully laid, detailed lesson plans with precision
      b. ___   designing lesson plans and learning strategies without necessarily carrying all of them out

27.   a. ___   logical people
      b. ___   feeling people

28.   a. ___   being free to do things on the spur of the moment
      b. ___   knowing well in advance what I am expected to do

29.   a. ___   being the center of attention
      b. ___   being reserved

30.   a. ___   imagining the non-existent
      b. ___   examining details of the actual

31.   a. ___   experiencing emotional situations, discussions, movies
      b. ___   using my ability to analyze situations

32.   a. ___   starting classes at a pre-arranged time
      b. ___   starting classes when all are comfortable or ready

✎   Provide teachers with the following scoring instructions: *Transfer your scores for each item of each pair to the appropriate blanks. Be careful to check the* a *and* b *letters to be sure you are recording scores in the right blank spaces. Then total the scores for each dimension.*

Personal Style Inventory Scoring Sheet

Instructions: Transfer your scores for each item of each pair to the appropriate blanks. Be careful to check the *a* and *b* letters to be sure you are recording scores in the right blank spaces. Then total the scores for each dimension.

I	E	N	S
1b. _____	1a. _____	2a. _____	2b. _____
5a. _____	5b. _____	6b. _____	6a. _____
9a. _____	9b. _____	10a. _____	10b. _____
13a. _____	13b. _____	14a. _____	14b. _____

17a. _____	17b. _____	18a. _____	18b. _____
21b. _____	21a. _____	22a. _____	22b. _____
25b. _____	25a. _____	26b. _____	26a. _____
29b. _____	29a. _____	30a. _____	30b. _____
TOTAL I _____	TOTAL E _____	TOTAL N _____	TOTAL S _____

T	**F**	**P**	**J**
3a. _____	3b. _____	4a. _____	4b. _____
7a. _____	7b. _____	8a. _____	8b. _____
11a. _____	11b. _____	12a. _____	12b. _____
15b. _____	15a. _____	16a. _____	16b. _____
19b. _____	19a. _____	20b. _____	20a. _____
23b. _____	23a. _____	24b. _____	24a. _____
27a. _____	27b. _____	28a. _____	28b. _____
31b. _____	31a. _____	32b. _____	302a. _____
TOTAL T _____	TOTAL F _____	TOTAL P _____	TOTAL J _____

Personal Style Inventory Interpretation Sheet

Letters on the score sheet stand for:

I Introversion	E Extroversion	N Intuition	S Sensing
T Thinking	F Feeling	P Perceiving	J Judging

The likely interpretation of point totals:

20–21   Balance in the strengths of the dimensions.

22–24   Some strength in the dimension; some weakness in the other member of the pair.

25–29   Definite strength in the dimension; definite weakness in the other member of the pair.

30–40   Considerable strength in the dimension, considerable weakness in the other member of the pair.

Your typology is those four dimensions for which you had scores of 22 or more, although the relative strengths of all the dimensions actually constitute your typology. Scores of 20 or 21 show relative balance in a pair so that either member could be part of the typology.

Dimensions of the Typology

The following four pairs of dimensions are present to some degree in all teachers. It is the extremes that are described here. The strength of a dimension is indicated by the score for that dimension and will determine how closely the strengths and weaknesses described fit the teacher's personality.

Introversion-Extroversion   Teachers more introverted than extroverted tend to make decisions somewhat independently of constraints and prodding from the situation, school culture, other teachers or administrators. They are quiet, diligent at working alone, and seem socially reserved. They may dislike being interrupted while working and may tend to forget names and faces.

Extroverted teachers are attuned to school culture, other teachers, students and administrators, endeavoring to make decisions congruent with demands and expectations. Extroverted teachers are outgoing, socially free, interested in variety and in working in teams. An extroverted teacher may become impatient with long, slow tasks and does not mind being interrupted by people.

Intuition-Sensing   The intuitive teacher prefers possibilities, theories, the overall, invention, and the new; and becomes bored with nitty-gritty details, the concrete and actual, and facts unrelated to concepts. The intuitive teacher thinks and discusses in spontaneous leaps of intuition that may leave out or neglect details. Problem solving comes easily for this individual, although there may be a tendency to make errors of fact.

The sensing teacher prefers the concrete, real, factual, structured, tangible, the here-and-now; and becomes impatient with theory and the abstract, mistrusting intuition. The sensing teacher thinks in careful, detail-by-detail accuracy, remembering real facts, making few errors of fact, but possibly missing a conception of the overall.

Feeling-Thinking   The feeler makes judgments about life, people, occurrences, and things based on empathy, warmth, and personal values. As a consequence, feelers are more interested in people and feelings than in impersonal logic, analysis, and things. Feelers are interested in conciliation and harmony more than in being on top or achieving impersonal goals. The feeler gets along well with people in general.

The thinker makes judgments about life, people, occurrences, and things based on logic, analysis, and evidence, avoiding the irrationality of making decisions based on feelings and values. As a result, the thinker is more interested in logic, analysis, and verifiable conclusions than in empathy, values, and personal warmth. The thinker may step on others' feelings and needs without realizing it, neglecting to take into consideration the feelings of others.

Perceiving-Judging The perceiver is a gatherer, always wanting to know more before deciding, holding off decisions and judgments. As a consequence, the perceiver is open, flexible, adaptive, non-judgmental, able to see and appreciate all sides of issues. However, perceivers are also difficult to pin down and may be indecisive and non-committal, becoming involved in so many tasks that do not reach closure that they may become frustrated at times. Even when they finish tasks, perceivers will tend to look back at them and wonder whether they are satisfactory or could have been done another way. The perceiver wishes to roll with life rather than change it.

The judge is decisive, firm and sure, setting goals and sticking to them. The judge wants to close books, make decisions, and get on to the next project. When a project does not yet have closure, judges will leave it behind and go on to new tasks and not look back.

Communication Skills: Self-Disclosure

In every process of communication, teachers are both senders and receivers of messages, verbally and non-verbally, by act and by omission. It is impossible not to communicate. Think of the powerful message that may be read in the phone call not returned or the letter not answered. But it is often appallingly difficult to communicate exactly' what we intended to say. The next sections proceed from (1) the Johari Window as a useful model for conceptualizing the communication process, to (2) the skills of self-disclosure necessary for the teacher to send clear messages to students, parents and others, then (3) the listening skills necessary for the teacher to receive communication, and finally (4) the skills of giving and receiving feedback necessary to sustain communication at a more than superficial level. This will enable teachers to better communicate to students, parents and other educators.

1. The Johari Window

The Johari Window (named for its originators, psychologists Joseph Luft and Harry Ingham) offers a convenient way for understanding the skills involved in interpersonal communication.

I. The Public Area contains the data known both to the self and to others,

	KNOWN TO SELF	NOT KNOWN TO SELF
KNOWN TO OTHERS	I Public area	II Blind Spot
NOT KNOWN TO OTHERS	III Hidden area	IV Unknown area

e.g., that I have brown hair, that I am male or female, that I speak English.

II. The Blind Spot contains data known to the others but not to the self, e.g., how the back of my head looks, that there is a spot on the seat of my pants, some facial mannerism of which I am unaware.

III. The Hidden Area contains certain things known to the self but not to the others, either because there has been no opportunity to reveal them or because I really wish to keep them hidden: e.g., where I was born, my mother's maiden name; or, in the second category, my age, that I have three false teeth, how much I earn.

IV. The Unknown Area is the wellspring of energy, creativity, and surprise, for it holds all the potentialities that are known neither to the self nor to the other. This material is below the level of conscious awareness, but some elements of it may emerge in a free, open and supportive interchange.

The larger the public area, the easier it is for a staff to work together, since more of the skills and resources of the teachers are available for the task at hand. The larger the public area in a relationship between teachers, the greater the possibility for closeness and trust. The public area can be enlarged by self-disclosure.

Two sets of skills are necessary for successful "self-disclosure," that is, when a teacher begins to share his or her perceptions, feelings and thoughts openly. The two sets of skills necessary for successful self-disclosure include: (1) the skills of expression, of sending clear messages on the part of the discloser; and (2) the skills of listening, of receiving messages sensitively and accurately on the part of the other.

The other way to enlarge the public area is through feedback, that is, through the other revealing to the self some of the contents of the blind spot, specifically, how the self is perceived by the other. Feedback allows teachers "to see themselves as others see them"; it can tell them what effect their behavior is having on others. Again, two sets of skills are necessary: those for giving and those for receiving feedback.

Any change in one area will affect all the others. It takes energy to hide or to be blind to behavior which is involved in an interaction. Therefore, self-disclosure and feedback tend to release energy and to enhance freedom of action. With a staff that has a high degree of mutual trust and openness, the release of energies may tap into the unknown area, producing flashes of insight and creativity previously unsuspected.

Objective: Teachers will be able to practice using the Johari Window in order to gain new insights into their relationships with others.

- ❧ Have teachers form groups of three.
- ❧ Ask each teacher to write down two things in the public area that each other teacher knows about them.
- ❧ Have each write down something from their hidden area. Assure them that they are free to choose what they wish to reveal and should do only what they are comfortable with.
- ❧ Each teacher may now tell the other two something they may not know about her/himself. Remind them that all are free to choose what they want to say and how much risk they feel comfortable in taking.
- ❧ Ask each group to discuss the following questions: *What happened in your trio? any insights? surprises? How comfortable/uncomfortable were you in self-disclosure? in giving feedback?*
- ❧ An additional step for a staff whose teachers know each other fairly well: Have each teacher draw a Johari Window for the other two in the trio, filling in the windows with data observed during the group interaction. Teachers can then exchange drawings and discuss differences in perceptions, feelings.

2. Describing One's Self and Others

Objectives: (1) Teachers will be able to encourage free association in themselves and others. (2) Teachers will be able to use free association. (3) Teachers will be able to use free association as a means of increasing self-awareness. (4) Teachers will be able to use free association as a means of building trust.

- ❧ Have teachers stand up and move around the room in silence. After a few moments, they should choose someone they would like to get to know better. No one should assist teachers in making this choice.
- ❧ Pairs find comfortable seating, then spend two or three minutes writing a "free association" description of themselves. (See Automatic Writing, earlier, for detailed instructions.)
- ❧ Ask the teachers to repeat the free association process—this time writing a description of the partner.

    ✄   Have teachers share their writing and discuss the following questions: *Were there similarities and differences between self-description and description by your partner? Did any parts of your partner's description of you sound familiar? Did any of it seem inaccurate? How do you feel at the end of this exercise? Do you notice any difference as compared to when you began?*

    ✄   Allow time for sharing of insights and comments in the total group.

3. Sharing Secrets
This exercise requires a trained facilitator.

Objective: Teachers will be able to experience self-disclosure as freeing.

    ✄   Plan to work on this exercise with no more than 10 teachers at a time. To preserve anonymity, provide identical pencils and cards or slips of paper for each teacher. Have each teacher write down on the card a secret about himself or herself that has rarely or never been shared with anyone. Make it clear that no names are to be used. The cards are folded and placed in a container. The facilitator draws one at a time and reads it aloud.

    ✄   The group of teachers discusses each secret as read, without breaching anonymity. There is a freeing aspect simply in being able to share a secret anonymously. Moreover, quite often the teacher discovers that something she or he has been hiding as a "dark secret" is not regarded as "dark" by others, or is something which others in the group also have experienced.

    ✄   At the end of the exercise, the cards are gathered up and destroyed.

Communication Skills: Active Listening

Communication is a two-fold process, depending for its success on sensitive receiving of messages as much as on clear sending. The skills of active listening are the skills of the receiver. It is not enough to be within earshot and let the message wash over one. Listening is an active process, demanding focused attention, awareness of non-verbals, careful checking of one's perceptions. This section provides teachers with an introduction to some of these skills.

1. Mirroring
Objectives: (1) Teachers will increase their awareness of non-verbals. (2) Teachers will increase their attentiveness to others.

* Have teachers form pairs and stand facing each other.
* Ask one teacher to take on the role of the sender of messages, and the other to become the mirror. The sender can do anything he or she wishes—pretend to be getting dressed, express feelings, make faces, whatever. The "mirror" attempts to accurately reflect whatever the sender does.
* Have the teachers reverse roles and repeat the exercise.
* Have the teachers discuss the following questions: *How did you feel as sender? as mirror? Does the sender think he or she was reflected accurately by the mirror? Did you learn anything about your attentiveness in this exercise? about other aspects of yourself?*

2. Making Contact with Others
Adapted from Andrew Panzarella, *Microcosm*.

Communication is a process of reaching out in order to make contact with others. But often we are ambivalent about contact: We want closeness, we want to be understood and to understand, but we also want privacy and fear intrusion.

Objective: Teachers will be able to explore their feelings about contact and private space.

* Ask teachers to arrange their chairs in a circle.
* Ask the teachers to close their eyes and in silence proceed to explore their space, stretching out hands and feet in all directions—up, down, left, right, forward, back—exploring their space as fully as possible, while still remaining seated.
* After three or four minutes of exploring space, have the teachers open their eyes and discuss:
  How close are you to the nearest teacher?
  Did anyone leave his or her chair somewhat outside the circle?
  Does this spatial arrangement reflect anything about the relationship of this teacher to the group?
  How did you feel when exploring your space with your arms and legs?
  Did you touch anyone else during your explorations? Did anyone touch you?
  How did you feel about touching or being touched? Did you feel you were intruding? Being intruded upon?

*Do you feel you have enough space? Do you feel others are crowding in
on you?*

*What did you think about the relation of physical distance to the ability
to make contact with others?*

3. Receiving Messages

Objective: Teachers will be able to increase their attentiveness to the sender.

- Have the teachers form circles of six to eight persons each.
- Each teacher takes a turn, giving his or her name and favorite color, using an "-ing" verb to describe some personal characteristic and mentioning a current concern.
- Then have the teachers turn their chairs around, so that they have their backs to each other, and write down what they remember.
- Have the teachers turn back to the circle and share what they have written in light of the following questions: *How much were you able to remember of what each teacher said? What helped? What hindered?*

4. Perception Checking
This exercise requires a trained facilitator.

Objective: Teachers will be able to demonstrate increased awareness of the differences between observations and inferences.

- Invite the teachers to choose a partner whom they do not know very well.
- Have one teacher describe the other teacher drawing some inference from the observation, according to the following pattern:

  Describing Teacher: *I see that you are tapping your left foot, and I think that indicates tension. I think you may be feeling nervous in this situation. Is that so?*

  Described teacher responds: *Yes I am feeling somewhat nervous, but I wasn't aware of my foot.*

- Have teachers reverse roles and repeat.
- Ask the teachers to discuss the following: *How did you feel when your partner described you? What are some consequences of failing to check out perceptions?*
- Ask each teacher to write down how he or she feels about the discussion at that moment, i.e., positive or negative.
- Then have each teacher write down how he or she thinks the other is

feeling. Each teacher's self-evaluation is put on the board. The teachers are then polled: "How many guessed that Jane was feeling positive?"

* Have individual teachers then interview those whose feelings they misread to discover the cause of the misreading.

* Ask the teachers to discuss ways to improve accuracy and factors that prevent them from perceiving others accurately.

* This exercise can be repeated several times, using statements about which there is a difference of opinion among the teachers, so that teachers can improve their accuracy of perception.

5. Paraphrasing

Objective: Teachers will be able to develop skills in paraphrasing and empathizing.

* Have teachers form groups of three. Ask one teacher to discuss with another teacher a topic, such as:
  Some important things that have been happening in my life lately.
  What I like best about myself.
  Something I'm really concerned about right now.
  Something I'd like to change about myself.

* Ask the receiving teacher to be a sympathetic listener, drawing out the speaker, paraphrasing, and reflecting feelings. Have the third teacher observe the conversation, paying attention to clarity of expression, accuracy of paraphrasing and identification of feeling.

* After three to five minutes have the observer feed back observations.

* Continue the exercise until each teacher has had a turn in all three roles.

* Have the teachers discuss the following questions:
  What difficulties did you experience in each role?
  What barriers do you observe to effective listening?
  How effective was your self-expression?
  To what degree did the listener demonstrate the behavior of a good listener?

6. Mixed Messages

Often teachers need to recognize and respond to mixed messages when gestures or body language or tone of voice seems contrary to what a person is saying. In this case, verbal content seems to contradict body language. Understandably, mixed messages are often confusing to the teacher who needs the skill to disentangle the two messages and check perceptions with the sender.

Objective: Teachers will be able to develop skill in disentangling mixed messages.

- Have each teacher choose a partner and sit facing him/her. Ask them to begin a conversation, with one teacher taking care to cancel his or her statements non-verbally—by a laugh, tone of voice, gesture or a wink.
- Have them reverse roles, with the other doing the non-verbal canceling.
- Ask the teachers to discuss the following questions:
  How did it feel to be on the receiving end of a mixed message.
  What means did you use to cancel your messages?
  Did either of you use a verbal message where one part cancels the other?
  How did you attempt to deal with the mixed message?
- Have the teachers repeat the experiment, but this time ask the receiver to consciously try to separate the two parts of the message and either (1) ask for clarification—"What are you telling me?" or (2) indicate clearly which part he or she is responding to.

7. Identifying Another's Feelings
Adapted from Thomas Gordon, *P.E.T.: Parenting Effectiveness Training*

Objective: Teachers will become more skilled in identifying another's feelings when they are not expressed directly.

- Give the following handout to the teachers and have them write down the feelings they identify as those that are the basis of the statements.

Handout: Recognizing Feelings
Read each item separately, trying to listen carefully for feelings. Then write the feeling or feelings you perceive. Discard the content and write in only the feeling— usually one or several words. Some statements may contain several different feelings; write all the main feelings you perceive.

A student comes to you and says:	Your feeling(s):
1. I don't know what's wrong.	_____
I'm just not getting anywhere.	_____
Maybe I should just quit trying.	_____

2. For all the attention anyone pays
   me in this place, I might as well
   not be here.

   _____
   _____
   _____

3. If things don't improve around
   here, I'll look for a new job.

   _____
   _____

4. That teacher is awful. She didn't
   teach me a thing.

   _____
   _____

5. Can't you see I'm busy?

   _____

6. The deadline for this term paper
   is just not realistic.

   _____
   _____

7. I'd sure like to go, but I just
   can't call her up. What if she'd
   laugh at me?

   _____
   _____
   _____

8. I'm putting in a lot of time
   practicing, but I don't get the
   result Anne does.

   _____
   _____
   _____

9. Why did old Mr. Sawyer make
   me stay after class? I wasn't the
   only one who was talking.

   _____
   _____
   _____

10. I'd like to go on to college, but
    I don't know if I can make the
    grade.

    _____
    _____
    _____

* Have teachers form pairs and share the results.

Communication Skills: Giving and Receiving Feedback

The notion of "feedback" comes from the field of automation. Feedback is any information about the result of a process, especially when used as input to maintain the output within certain limits. Thus, a thermostat gives feedback to a furnace on how well it is heating the house, and this information either turns the furnace on or off automatically.

In the process of interpersonal communication, feedback means giving the receiver information on how his or her behavior is affecting you. To return to the Johari Window, feedback is information coming from Area II, the Blind Spot. However, unlike the automation process, the communication process requires choices both on the part of the giver and the receiver of feedback. The following "Notes on Feedback" indicate the main elements to be considered.

Feedback is the communication to another person of information about how his or her behavior is affecting you. It is not a demand for change, but rather the giving of some relevant information. It leaves the receiver free to decide what use, if any, he or she will make of the information. Feedback helps a person to learn from experience; it enables him or her to check on how well his or her behavior matches his or her intentions; it increases his or her options.

Teachers often view feedback as a form of grading and see it as their responsibility to tell students what they are doing wrong. Students learn very early that it is not OK to make a mistake and learn from it.

The following guidelines indicate more and less effective ways of giving feedback to students and can help teachers allow students to learn from experience.

Feedback is more effective when:

1.   Students ask for feedback or there are other clear indications that the student is ready for it.

2.   It is descriptive. A clear report of the facts rather than a teacher's ideas about why things happened or what they mean. Teachers should use direct quotes and examples.

3.   It is specific. Teachers are clear and specific about the aspect of behavior they are giving feedback on.

4.   It is about behavior the student can modify.

5.   It is about behavior that the teacher can observe.

6.   It is recent. Usually, it is most useful when given at the earliest opportunity after the student's behavior.

7.   It is given at an appropriate time. It should be given when there is a good chance that the student can use it.

8.   It is given to be helpful. The teacher needs to consider his or her own motives in order to be certain that he/she is not acting out of personal needs.

9.   The teacher does not demand a change, but tries to make new data available to the student.

10. The teacher covers one point at a time.

Feedback is less effective when:

1. It is imposed. If not ready, the student will be apt not to hear it or will misinterpret it.
2. It is evaluative. Teachers need to evaluate the student's work, not the student.
3. It is general.
4. It is about behavior not under the student's control.
5. It is about motives or intentions.
6. It is about ancient history. Feedback on a student's past behavior is less effective than feedback about recent behavior and may trigger defense mechanisms that students use to defend themselves when their parents punish them and bring up the past.
7. It is given at an inappropriate time. If the student is very busy, preoccupied, or depressed she/he is not apt to hear it.
8. It is for the teacher. Feedback is not for the purpose of enabling the teacher to relieve anxieties or to demonstrate superiority and control over the student.
9. It is demanding a change.
10. It is an overload.

For feedback to be effective, students need to learn how to best receive it. The following points should be made to students frequently so that they can make effective use of feedback.

Points for Students

1. Remember you are free to decide what use, if any, you make of the information.
2. Remember that feedback helps you to learn from experience. It enables you to check on how you are coming across, how clearly you are expressing your feelings, and how well your behavior matches your intentions.
3. It is helpful to ask for feedback and to mention specific points on which you would like feedback.
4. It is helpful to check whether you have heard accurately what has been said.
5. Let your teacher know if you find the feedback helpful or not.
6. Share your feelings with your teacher, but try not to get defensive or get into an argument about the content. Remember that all you need to do is to take this bit of information under consideration.

1. Positive Feedback

Objective: Teachers will become better skilled in giving and receiving positive messages.

- Have each teacher bring in a shoe box and put it in front of her or him to serve as a mailbox.

- Tell the teachers that they have twenty minutes in which to write messages. Have them address each message to a specific person by name. Give them the following instructions: *Write in the first person; "I see ... I like ... " Be honest, clear and precise about something positive you have observed in the other teacher, why you are glad to work with her or him, etc. Whether you sign your name or not is your choice.*

- Have teachers deliver messages and have each teacher read his or her own.

- Ask the teachers to discuss the following questions:
  What feelings come up when you are acknowledged positively?
  Was it difficult for anyone to receive positive feedback?
  Did you find yourself spontaneously thinking, "Yes, but ... ?"
  In trying to be specific in writing your positive message, did you become aware of something you had not noticed before?
  Did you find it easier to give or receive positive feedback?
  Are any of the messages ambiguous? If the message is signed, ask the sender to clarify.

2. Symbolic Feedback

Objective: Teachers will develop skill in expressing feedback symbolically.

- Ask each teacher to take a turn at becoming the focus of the group.

- Have other teachers think of a car or flower which they associate with the receiver of the feedback.

- Have the teachers discuss the following questions: *How do you feel about being associated with the car or flower? What reasons did the givers of the feedback have for their choice?*

3. Requesting Feedback

A trained facilitator is required for this exercise.

Objectives: (1) Teachers will become more at ease in requesting feedback. (2) Teachers will develop skills in giving feedback.

- Call for three volunteers. Let the teachers know that each volunteer will ask the group for feedback on the impression he or she is making on the group.

* Have the volunteers ask for feedback.
* Ask the group to think of ways in which any two of the three are like each other and different from the third. Have the teachers take a few minutes to write down as many points as they can in all possible combinations of the three people taken two at a time.
* Then have the teachers take turns giving their perceptions of the similarities and differences.
* Have the three receivers of feedback then respond by: *Asking for clarifications, if any are needed. Sharing their feelings.*
* Ask for three other volunteers and continue with the exercise until all who wish to volunteer have had the opportunity to do so.

4. Non-Verbal Feedback

Objective: Teachers will develop skill in expressing feelings toward another non-verbally.

* Ask one teacher to volunteer to act as "sculptor." Other teachers are to act as "clay." One or two teachers are detailed to be "cameras," noting gestures and postures.
* Have the sculptor put each teacher in position, according to her or his perceptions of their closeness or distance from each other, their role in the group, their characteristic gestures and posture.
* Ask the teachers to discuss: *The "camera's" feedback; their observations. Their feelings and perceptions, first of their own position, then of others in the sculpture.*
* The experience may be repeated with another volunteer as sculptor.

5. Video Feedback

Oh, wad some power the giftie gie us/To see ourselves as ithers see us ...

The VCR has quite literally answered Robert Burns's prayer. Most teachers experience shock the first time they receive feedback from a video tape, so accustomed are they to viewing their behavior from the inside out, rather than to perceive themselves from the outside.

Objective: For teachers to learn to utilize feedback from videotape.

* Have two or three teachers role play a situation or engage in a

Directions: In the sheet on the opposite page, choose one teacher whom you are going to observe during the interaction. The sheet provides two columns, one for the speaker, the other for the listener/responder. In the top half of each column, record the non-verbal behaviors of your teacher as he or she speaks and listens using check marks and/or short phrases. In the bottom half of each column, record verbal behaviors.

OBSERVER'S WORK SHEET
1. Non-Verbal Behavior

LISTENER/RESPONDER	SPEAKER
eye contact	
physical distance	
body direction (toward or away from the other)	
body gestures (withdrawn ... aggressive, neutral ... supportive)	
body movement (rigid ... fluid)	

2. Verbal Behavior

Door Openers ("I see ...," "Tell me more ...")	Speaks for self? for others? ("I feel,", "I think," or "We feel")
Paraphrases content ("I hear you saying ...")	States points clearly
Checks own perceptions ("I think you feel ...")	Gives examples
Describes behavior of others (descriptive, not evaluative language)	
Shares own feelings	

discussion on some topic that is personally involving, e.g., I am happiest when ... "The thing that turns me off most is ... Something I do well ... Something I'd like to change about myself ...

* Videotape the teachers, but continue the interaction long enough so that the teachers have ceased to be aware of the camera.

* Have the other teachers act as observers, using the Observer's Sheet on the next page .

* Play the tape and have the teachers make notes on their own behavior; and have three observers add their notes to the teachers' work sheets.

* Have the teachers discuss the following questions: *How did the teachers feel on seeing and/or hearing themselves? Any surprises? What did the teachers notice about their own communication styles? What did observers notice? Did observers pick up additional points from the tape?*

* You may want to replay portions of the tape for close analysis. You may also wish to re-enact part or all of the original situation, with teachers trying alternative behaviors.

Caring For Students

Caring requires an awareness of the student's needs and a willingness to help meet them. Caring requires time, openness and commitment. Relationships are never static; they are flexible and require teachers never to stop learning new ways of responding to students.

1. Exploring Definitions of Caring

Objectives: (1) Teachers will be able to analyze various definitions of caring and closeness. (2) Teachers will be able to identify elements they may wish to include in their own definition of caring.

Materials: The Credo for Relationships by Thomas Gordon. *The Credo for Relationships* by Virginia Satir.

Thomas Gordon's Credo for Relationships

You and I are in a relationship which I value and want to keep. Yet each of us is a separate person with his own unique needs and the right to try to meet those needs. I will try to be genuinely accepting of your behavior, both when you are trying to meet your needs and when you are having problems meeting your needs.

When you share your problems, I will try to listen in an accepting and understanding way that will facilitate your finding your own solutions rather than depending upon mine. When you have a problem because my behavior is interfering with your meeting your needs, I encourage you to tell me openly and honestly how you are feeling. At those times, I will listen and then try to modify my behavior.

However, when your behavior interferes with me meeting my own needs, thus causing me to feel unaccepting of you, I will tell you as openly and honestly as I can exactly how I am feeling, trusting that you respect my needs enough to listen and try to modify your behavior.

At those times when neither of us can modify his/her behavior to meet the needs of the other, thus finding that we have a conflict-of-needs in our relationship, let us commit ourselves to resolve each such conflict without ever resorting to the use of either my power or yours to win at the expense of the other losing. I respect your needs but I must also respect my own. Consequently, let us strive always to search for solutions to our inevitable conflicts that will be acceptable to both of us. In this way, your needs will be met, but so will mine—no one will lose; both will win. As a result, you can continue to develop as a person through meeting your needs, but so can I. Our relationship can always be a healthy one because it will be mutually satisfying. Thus, each of us can become what he is capable of being, and we can continue to relate to each other in mutual respect, friendship, love and peace.

Virginia Satir's Credo for Relationships

I want to love you without clutching
appreciate you without judging
join you without invading
invite you without demanding
leave you without guilt
criticize you without blaming
and help you without insulting.
If I can have the same from you
then we can truly meet
and enrich each other.

* Have the teachers read the Credos by Gordon and Satir, therapists who have had extensive experience in helping people improve their relationships.
* Ask the teachers to choose two statements which most appeal to them and to try to identify the elements which each writer regards as important in a caring relationship.
* Have the teachers form small groups and discuss the following questions: *What assumptions is each writer making about human beings, about change, about solitude, about commitment and accountability? What expectations would each have of "the other?" Which elements, assumptions, expectations do you share?*

2. Developing a Personal Credo

Each teacher has his or her idea of a healthy and positive teacher-student relationship. It is important to make explicit assumptions and expectations and to test them against reality.

Objectives: (1) Teachers will be able to clarify their assumptions about caring and their expectations of themselves and students. (2) Teachers will be able to check the realism of their expectations.

* Have the teachers write their own credo for relationships with students, taking into account in some way the following factors: *time, relationship to the future, openness to change, accountability, control, conflict, commitment to one's personal growth, privacy*
* Have the teachers reflect on their credo and make a list of assumptions and expectations they have of themselves and students.
* Have the teachers form small groups and discuss the following questions: *Are my assumptions well founded? Are my expectations realistic?*

3. Expressing Wants and Needs Clearly

This skill is particularly important for teachers to sustain a caring relationship.

Objective: Teachers will be better able to express needs and wants clearly and specifically.

* Have the teachers form small groups. Then give each teacher a slip of paper, containing a vaguely worded need or want, e.g., "I want you to listen to me."

* In each group have one teacher read a slip of paper. Then ask the group to meet that need for that teacher.
* Have the others take turns reading their slip of paper but have them make the need more specific, and hence achievable, by asking, "Do you mean you want me to tell you what I hear you saying?" etc., until they get at least three positive answers.
* Have the teachers discuss the following questions: *How did you feel when you first heard the request? Do you make such requests in your daily life or meet them from others?*

Dealing with Conflict

Conflict is an inevitable part of human life, a necessary condition for growth and for the development of mutually rewarding relationships. Teachers will have conflict with students, parents, administrators and each other. However, to deal with conflict creatively and constructively requires skill. This section presents exercises and analysis toward that end.

1. Attitudes Toward Conflict

Objective: Teachers will be able to get in touch with their dominant attitudes toward conflict.

* Have teachers form small groups and brainstorm a list of words they associate with conflict.
* Have each group go through their list, evaluating the words as positive or negative. In most groups, the list will be overwhelmingly negative.
* Ask the teachers to discuss the following questions: *Why do we view conflict as negative? What is the worst thing you can think of as happening as a result of a conflict with a student? Can you see any advantages in conflict?*

2. Understanding Conflict

Conflict means to come into opposition with another and to use your power to attempt to "win."

Objective: Teachers will be able to gain skill in analyzing conflict.

The following are examples of common outcomes of conflict:

Win/Lose. This situation is the predominant form in our culture, where we tend to define conflict situations—whether in sports, education, business or even personal relations—as competition for scarce resources, the trophy, the scholarship, the job. A Win/Lose approach leads easily into a negative situation, since the anger and resentment of the loser does not disappear, but simply goes underground to emerge later as backlash. Thus, in a quarrel between students, when the teacher intervenes to establish Johnny's ownership of a pencil, Tommy's resentment may express itself by breaking the pencil so that neither one can use it. Fortunately, we need not define every conflict situation as competition for scarce goods. Because human beings are basically interdependent, the achievement of my goal may include the achievement of yours. Moreover, when we have identified a common goal, conflict, if openly surfaced and honestly faced, can improve both planning and implementation. More alternatives are likely to emerge from opposed views on how to proceed, and the resulting solution is apt to be better than that which any single participant could have produced.

Conflict is an inescapable part of human life. As soon as there are two people, there are two viewpoints and two sets of needs which are bound to rub against each other some of the time. In any organized human effort, we must set up different roles and responsibilities, hence different needs and priorities.

It would seem, then, that we do not have a choice about whether or not to encounter conflict; since conflict is inevitable, our only choice is how to deal with it. There are three basic ways of handling conflict:

1. Moving away from it either by total denial, or by suppressing or minimizing differences; or by distracting ourselves and the other by changing the subject; or by giving in, surrendering or placating. Partial or total suppression of conflict, generally leads to physical and/or psychological sickness for the weaker party, or to manipulation and emotional blackmail which interferes with the relationship, and/or to an enlarged blind spot on the part of the more powerful party, and eventually an explosion of suppressed resentment in some form of aggression.

2. Moving against the other, fighting back in an attempt to overpower the other. This mode produces escalating feelings of anger and hostility and escalating violence of actions and reactions.

3. Moving toward the conflict in an open confrontation. Confrontation is a way of using opposition constructively, trying to move from a Win/Lose situation toward a compromise situation. Confrontation requires a willingness to communicate, to explore alternatives and to increase options.

- Have the teachers form small groups, and ask one teacher in each group to identify a person with whom they are having a conflict.

- Ask the teacher to indicate how much they care about their relationship with that person on a scale of 1–10, 10 meaning they have strong feelings of wanting to maintain the relationship; 1 meaning they have relatively little investment in maintaining the relationship.

- Then on a scale of 1–10, have them indicate how important to them is the issue about which they are in conflict—10 meaning the issue is extremely important and they think about it night and day; 1 meaning the issue itself is relatively unimportant.

- Pass out the chart opposite and have them indicate where their conflict lies in order to assess the nature of the conflict in their life.

- Now have them, as accurately as possible, determine how the person they are in conflict with might answer the same question and indicate what they think his/her position would be on the chart.

- Have each group reflect on what must be done to move the conflict into either the compromise or collaborative areas on the chart.

3. Deciding Whether to Confront

Objectives: (1) Teachers will be able to assess strengths and weaknesses of their own position. (2) Teachers will be able to frame a strategy.

- Have teachers form pairs and discuss a situation in which they wish to confront another.

- Have them act as a consultant and discuss the following questions:
  Are you willing to take the risk?
  When do you plan the confrontation?
  Is the other in a state to listen?
  Where do you plan it?
  Are you confronting behavior or motives?
  Can you be clear, concrete?
  Have you looked at your own motives—are you fairly sure you are not meeting your own needs at the expense of the other?
  How much are you willing to invest in working through the confrontation?

4. How to Handle Being Confronted

Objective: Teachers will develop skill in responding non-defensively to attacks.

- Have the teachers form small groups and role play some of the following common attacks:

FIELD OF CONFLICT

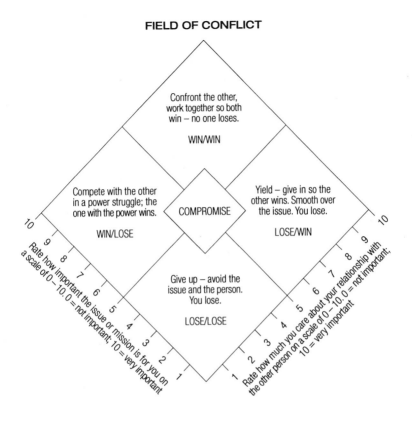

"*You are always late!*" (*Young woman to her date*)

"*You always hog the limelight!*" (*Wife to husband on way home from party*)

"*Can't you ever get things straight?*" (*Employer to Employee*)

"*It was not your place to make that suggestion.*" (*One committee member to another after a meeting*)

✖ Have the teachers repeat the role playing using the following methods:

Empathize with the other's feelings.

Paraphrase what the other is saying ("I hear you saying … "). Be sure you have the message clear before you agree or disagree.

Ask questions to clarify what specifically you are doing that is the occasion for the other to call you "selfish," "arrogant," or whatever.

Either ask for an example or ask "Do you mean … ?"

Try to maintain a problem-solving attitude: you want to learn from the other's observations, feelings, wants.

EXERCISES FOR TEACHERS TO DEVELOP IMAGINAL SKILLS

Imaginal Skills: The blend of fantasy and feeling that enables teachers to combine images and ideas in new ways, to see alternatives, to change conventional ways of doing things, to remedy deficiencies. Imaginal skills emerge naturally from the instrumental ability to process and act on information effectively and the interpersonal ability to see oneself and others accurately which facilitates communication, understanding and cooperation.

Examples of Imaginal Skills for Teachers

1. The ability to "break set," i.e. to identify one's unconscious assumptions about the limits in a situation.
2. The ability to defer judgment, to avoid the habitual response.
3. The ability to tolerate ambiguity.
4. The ability to daydream and brainstorm creatively.
5. The ability to look at a problem from a fresh angle, redefining it in new ways.
6. Fluency in making fresh associations and perceiving connections.
7. Fluency in communicating verbally.
8. Awareness of and sensitivity to the natural environment.
9. Sensitivity to language, to the origins and meaning of words.
10. Fluency in communicating through poetry and drama.
11. The ability to generate alternative solutions to problems.
12. The ability to put together existing elements or data in new ways.
13. The ability to imagine behavioral alternatives for oneself, alternative ways of expressing one's values.
14. The ability to elaborate on an idea or plan, developing the details.
15. The ability to make alternative long-term plans for oneself.
16. The ability to make alternative long-term plans for a group or organization.
17. The ability to see the consequences of alternative courses of action.
18. The ability to prioritize among alternatives.
19. The ability to use brainstorming with a group to generate alternative solutions.
20. The ability to call upon a variety of alternatives in the heat of tension or conflict situations.
21. The ability to help others generate new ideas.

All teachers have imagination, the power that enables them to call up images out of past experience, to rearrange and combine them in new ways, to see alternatives, to remedy deficiencies, to change conventional ways of doing things. But many of us repress imaginative powers for fear of ridicule and lack of confidence in our own perceptions or we allow them to atrophy through disuse. Teachers seldom set about deliberately to develop Imaginal skills in themselves or their students and thus tend to conform to the environment rather than opening their eyes to new possibilities and taking the initiative to bring them about. Moreover, much of formal education tends to direct teachers' energies into what is called convergent thinking, that is, remembering and reproducing what is already known.

Teachers are trained to make the correct responses to pre-determined problems and are rewarded for "right answers." Of course, it is necessary for them to acquire skills in convergent thinking, but it is equally important to develop the capacity for its opposite, divergent thinking—the ability to create new wholes out of pre-existing elements, to explore the unstructured situation, to redefine the problem from a fresh angle, to generate the new, the unconventional, the original. Divergent thinking is open-ended in the sense that it invites the unexpected and the unpredictable. Imaginal skills depend upon divergent thinking. Paul Torrance distinguishes four characteristics of divergent thinking:

1. Flexibility, the ability to see with a fresh pair of eyes, to shift from one perspective to another, quite literally to move to a different standpoint.
2. Fluency, an abundant flow of words, images, ideas.
3. Originality, the capacity to produce fresh responses, arising out of each person's unique perspective, personal history and reactions.
4. Elaboration, the ability to develop an idea or image, to make connections and fill in details.

However, before teachers can even begin to develop these various aspects of divergent thinking, they need to break through the barriers imposed both by their internal censors and the censorship of the environment. It takes courage to be creative. Just as soon as a teacher has a new idea, he or she becomes a minority of one, a position that most teachers avoid almost by instinct. They have learned to be afraid of failing, of being different, or of being laughed at. If by chance a stray fantasy escapes internal censorship, it is quickly put in its place by friends, fellow teachers or administrators. Therefore, this section begins with exercises intended "to break set," that is, to free up the imagination and to increase one's confidence in one's own perceptions, desires and dreams. When using this material with groups of teachers, particular care should be taken to set an open and supportive atmosphere, giving free rein to fantasy and "wild ideas," encouraging free associations and withholding judgment and evaluation until the final stages of the process.

In each section, the exercises are arranged in a developmental sequence, moving from simpler to more complex tasks and from direct sensory experience to more abstract considerations of possibilities, values, courses of action and social systems. The arrangement also proceeds from more structured to less structured starting points. In fact, some of the beginning exercises are instances of convergent rather than divergent thinking, e.g., the various puzzle exercises which admit of only one correct solution. These have been included to serve as a kind of intermediate step between the convergent and divergent modes, since their solution requires some breaking of set and/or flexibility and thus can help to build both skills and confidence. Initially, opening up too large a space for the imagination may prove bewildering or overwhelming. Thus, it is more difficult for most teachers to respond to the directive to "write a story" than to respond to the directive to "write an ending to this story." The addition of boundaries or limiting conditions makes a project more tangible and imaginable. After individuals gain confidence in their own perceptions and fantasies, more open-ended projects can be used.

There is no section on originality as such. Each teacher occupies a unique place in the universe, has a unique personal history, and therefore is capable of unique expressions. The problem is to enable people to discover their own uniqueness, and the various means suggested here contribute toward that end. Originality is a fruit of fluency, flexibility, freedom and self-confidence.

Exercises to Free Up the Imagination

1. Force of Habit

Objective: Teachers will become aware of the discomfort or resistance in themselves to non-habitual behavior.

- Ask the teachers to clasp their hands and observe whether the right or left thumb is on top. Tally responses in the group. Experiments have shown that groups tend to divide approximately in half in this habitual response. The teachers began to fold their hands with the same thumb on top at a early age. It may have never occurred to them that there is another way to do it. Now, have them reclasp their hands, so that the other thumb is on top. Ask them to take a minute in silence to get in touch with how this feels: awkward? uncomfortable? strange? or equally comfortable either way?

* Have the teachers fold their arms and repeat the above steps.
* Have the teachers form cooperative groups and discuss the following questions: *Can you identify other areas in your life where you have strong, almost automatic responses? What are the advantages and disadvantages of these responses?*

2. Rules and Constraints

Objective: Teachers will identify their assumptions about the rules and constraints in a situation.

Resources: Two trained facilitators

* Divide the group of teachers into two parts, a small group of "haves" and a larger group of "have-nots." Announce that each group will have twenty minutes to consider its needs, desires and strategies before they meet together to negotiate.
* One facilitator leads the "haves" to a comfortable meeting space, equipped with easy chairs, cushions, refreshments, etc., announces that their task is to decide how to deal with the "have-nots," and that the facilitator is now taking on the role of observer.
* The other facilitator leads the "have-nots" to a small, crowded, uncomfortable space, e.g., a closet or a bathroom, announces that the task is to discuss the needs of the "have-nots" and that the facilitator is now taking on the role of observer.
* Have the observers record: *How do individual teachers respond to their situation? Who takes the initiative to lead the "have-nots" out of their confinement? How long does it take for someone to take this initiative? Do the "haves" take any initiatives with respect to the "have-nots"?*
* Now have each group discuss the following question: *What assumptions is each group making about the limits of their situation and about what behavior is appropriate?*

There is a proverb to the effect that in Germany everything is forbidden except what is explicitly permitted, while in England everything is permitted which is not explicitly forbidden. Did the teachers adopt the English or the German approach to the rules and regulations? What are the consequences of these two approaches?

3. Redefining the Problem

A problem is half-solved if it is properly stated. Often, too narrow a statement of a problem may constitute a "set" that prevents a solution. To break out of the set, teachers need to restate the problem as broadly as possible so as not to preclude any answer. To arrive at a broader statement, it is helpful for them to ask "Why?" "What am I ultimately trying to accomplish?"

Here are some common problems. See if by restating the problem in broader terms, teachers can come up with some possible solutions.

Objective: Teachers will develop skill in redefining problems in broader terms.

* Have the teachers form cooperative groups and discuss solutions to the following problems:

   a. A freight company based its charges on the weight of the merchandise. They were asked to ship boxes of textbooks that were so heavy it took four men to move them onto the scale. The manager did not have that much labor at her disposal and was puzzling over how to get the boxes onto the scale. Can you help her solve her problem?

   b. The teacher's work is unsatisfactory; the principal wonders how to fire him with minimum repercussions. How would you do it?

   c. Mary has been asked to chair the school improvement committee for her school, a very important and time-consuming task. She is deeply committed to the school and does not want to let anyone down, but given her teaching and graduate course work, she does not have the time to do the committee work properly. She is torn between refusing the assignment and burning the midnight oil in order to fulfill it. What should she do?

   d. John, a junior in college, is registered for a required course in his major which is given only in alternate years and meets Monday, Wednesday, and Friday at 10 A.M. He suffers from kidney disease and must spend every Monday morning at the hospital for a dialysis treatment, thus missing one-third of his classes. How can he rearrange his schedule?

Solutions:

   a. Not how do we get the boxes onto the scale, but how do we determine the freight charges? Weigh samples of standard sizes or use a roadside weigh station, weighing the empty and the loaded truck.

b. How to get the job done satisfactorily? Provide training for the teacher; or discuss his difficulties to get at the cause; assign him to other work for which he is better suited and hire a replacement.

c. In what other ways could she help the group reach its goals? Could she do other, less time-consuming work for the committee, thus giving someone else the opportunity to be chair? Or could she find another person to undertake the job? Or do it with a co-chairperson?

d. How can he meet the requirements for graduation? Through an alternative course? A special dispensation? Or can he meet the course requirement in an alternative way—through an independent study or a special project?

Exercises to Develop Flexibility

"Genius means little more than the faculty of
perceiving in an unhabitual way." —Wm. James

1. Making Pentaminoes
Adapted from Leonard Davidman, "On Educating the Imagination"

Objective: Teachers will develop skill in perceiving new relationships.

A pentamino is a two-dimensional figure made up of five one-inch squares, each of which has at least one full side in common with at least one other square. A pentamino is different from other pentaminoes when it cannot be constructed by sliding, rotating or flipping any of the others.

* Have the teachers form cooperative groups and construct as many different pentaminoes as they can.

* Have the teachers discuss the following questions: *What methods did you use in making pentaminoes? What helped you to discover new ones? What hindered?*

2. An Imaginary Ball Game
Objectives: (1) Teachers will develop a greater perception of non-verbal cues. (2) Teachers will develop skills to respond flexibly to changing cues.

* Have the teachers stand in a circle and have one teacher initiate play with an imaginary ball. Instruct the teachers to change the size and shape of the ball in the course of passing it to another.

* Have the teachers form cooperative groups and discuss the following

questions: *How did you feel during the game? Were you able to identify the kind of ball? to transform it? How comfortable were you with sudden shifts in size and shape?*

3. The Magic Box

Objectives: (1) Teachers will improve non-verbal expression. (2) Teachers will develop a greater perception of non-verbal cues. (3) Teachers will develop greater flexibility in responding to non-verbal cues.

- Have the teachers form a circle and ask one teacher to begin the exercise by miming the opening of an imaginary box, taking an object from it and passing it to someone in the circle. That person shows in mime that she or he grasps the identity of the object, then transforms it and passes it on. Allow each teacher to take a turn.
- Have the teachers form cooperative groups and discuss the following questions: *How did you feel during the game? Did transformations occur to you even when it was not your turn? Were you able to read all the clues?*

4. Making Fresh Associations

"Everything is relevant; making things relevant is the creative process." —W. J. J. Gordon

From earliest childhood, teachers have been taught to make certain associations between ideas or objects, e.g., bacon and eggs, dollars and cents, happy as a clam, bread and butter, clean as a whistle, and so on. Their speech and thoughts are full of such habitual, stereotyped patterns. One way to develop flexibility is to try consciously to relate unlike things.

Objectives: (1) Teachers will learn to develop fresh perceptions. (2) Teachers will develop greater ability to see the like in the unlike. (3) Teachers will develop the skills to generate similes and metaphors.

Below is a list of unusual comparisons, which point up likenesses in things belonging to very different categories:

Color likened to sound:
1. Black as a beating of drums.
2. Clouds as white as the bursting of a firecracker.

Natural object likened to manufactured:
1. Clouds like flying ice cream.
2. Hair like spaghetti.
3. A poodle like a fluffy dust mop.

Human to non-human:
1. Fingers like worms wriggling.
2. His anger was like a tornado.

Small to large:
1. The needle is the locomotive and the thread is the train.
2. A top spinning like the rings of Saturn.

* Have the teachers form cooperative groups and ask them to think of some sense impression (a color, sound, shape, taste, smell, touch) and generate a list of comparisons. Instruct them to let their imagination roam; and to try to find likeness across categories and between things that are usually considered to be totally unrelated.

* Have the teachers discuss the following questions: *Were you surprised by any of the comparisons? Did any of the comparisons seem forced? Did you find any methods that were helpful in generating new ideas?*

Developing Fluency

"The way to have a good idea is to have lots of ideas." —Linus Pauling

1. Observing a Common Object
Objective: Teachers will heighten their sensory awareness.

* Choose a common object—a ball-point pen, a lead pencil, a penny, a leaf, a stone. Each teacher should have the object at hand and be able to manipulate it. For three to five minutes, have each teacher examine the object and write down as many words or phrases as possible to describe it in whole or in part.

* Have the teachers form cooperative groups and share their lists, paying special attention to the differences. Instruct them to develop categories from the differences, i.e., the way the object looks, feels, sounds, smells, tastes, its shape, parts, materials, functions, etc.

* Have the teachers repeat the exercise with a second object. Ask them to discuss whether fluency improves with practice.

2. Developing Alternative Behaviors
Objective: Teachers will imagine a variety of possible self behaviors.

* Have the teachers form cooperative groups and ask each teacher to think of someone she or he is fond of and write down a list of ways to show positive feeling for this person.

* Have the teachers discuss and compare lists.
* Have the teachers discuss the following questions: *Did other teachers think of alternatives that did not occur to you, and vice versa? How do you feel about actually trying some of the new possibilities?*

3. Product Improvement
Adapted from E. Paul Torrance, *Torrance Tests of Creative Thinking.*

Objective: Teachers will develop greater fluency and flexibility.
* Have teachers form cooperative groups and ask each teacher to choose a familiar product—e.g., a desk calendar, a woman's handbag, the family bathtub, a briefcase—and make suggestions for product improvement. Have all teachers share their suggestions with their group.
* Have each group of teachers use the following questions to further discuss each product: *What would make it more useful? more interesting? more fun to use?*
* Now have each teacher choose a children's toy—a small stuffed animal, a coloring book, etc., and discuss the toy in light of the following questions: *What would make it more fun for children to play with? more stimulating to the child's imagination?*

4. Seeing Consequences
Adapted from E. Paul Torrance, *Torrance Tests of Creative Thinking.*

Objective: Teachers will develop skills to play with an idea and to entertain possibilities.
* Have the teachers form cooperative groups and discuss the following questions:
  Suppose all people had a third eye in the back of their head. What are some of the consequences that would result?
  What if clouds had strings?
  What if human beings had no thumbs?
  What if the earth were covered with a dense fog, extending down to two feet above the ground?
* Have each group record their answers to the questions and share those answers with the other groups. Ask the teachers to pay attention to unique and infrequent responses and analyze shifts in perspective and categories involved in the responses.

Exercises in Synthesis and Elaboration

"Briefly, the abilities believed to be the most relevant for creative thinking are
in two categories. One category is divergent production abilities. The other potential
source of creative talents is in the category of 'transformation' abilities, which pertain
to revising what one experiences or knows, thereby producing new forms and patterns."
—J. P. Guilford

1. Making Up a Story

Objective: Teachers will acquire skill in synthesizing and elaborating already existing elements.

* Provide the teachers with a set of pictures, taken from magazines or photo files, preferably with some people in them. The number of pictures should be several times the number of teachers, so that each person has many options to choose from. Ask each teacher to select a picture which stirs some feeling in them, either of attraction or of distaste, and to make up a story about it.

* Have the teachers form cooperative groups and share the stories.

* Have the teachers discuss the following questions: *What helped to produce ideas? what hindered? Which stories were most detailed? Which were most original?*

* Repeat the exercise using a dramatic reading as a starting point, read a scene from a novel, play or short story, with a narrator and the various characters presenting briefly an initial situation.

* Now have each teacher write an ending to the story, novel or play.

2. Brainstorming

Objective: Teachers will learn a technique of brainstorming.

* Explain the following concept of brainstorming: *The purpose is to generate a profusion of ideas. The production of ideas can be improved when certain conditions are met, namely: a group effort—two heads are better than one; a free and open atmosphere which favors spontaneity; a scrupulous avoidance of judging anyone's contribution during the generating process.*

* Have the teachers form cooperative groups and have each group select a recorder. Explain that teachers should try to build on each other's ideas, using them as stimuli or starting points.

* Instruct the groups to brainstorm a solution to the following problem:

Suppose I were to be dropped off in the wilderness. What would I need to survive for a weekend? What would be the absolute minimum on which I could manage? (Or the group can choose a current problem).

- Ask one teacher in each group to serve as observer, whose responsibility it is to call the group on any evaluative language that creeps in during the generating process.

- When the brainstorming period is over, the group may evaluate the ideas in terms of their usefulness.

3. Constructing a Game

Objective: Teachers will learn to use brainstorming as an aid in synthesizing.

- Divide the teachers into teams of four or five persons each. Ask each team to construct a game that can be played with some common object—e.g., a ball, a cup, a rope—using brainstorming in arriving at a solution. The group may add additional conditions if they think that will aid the process, e.g., the number of players, the place, whether it is to be competitive or not, etc.

- Have each team instruct the other teams in its game and have the teams play the game.

- Have each team discuss the following questions: *Did many of the teams have similar ideas? Were the teachers able to build on each other's ideas? What helped, what hindered the process of construction?*

4. Writing a Poem

Objective: Teachers will expand their personal vision of the world.

"Children have a natural talent for writing poetry, and anyone who teaches them should know that," writes Kenneth Koch. "Teaching really is not the right word for what takes place: it is more like permitting the children to discover something they already have." Koch has been remarkably successful in helping many people to discover their talent for writing poetry, people who have never thought of themselves as poets, such as children in elementary schools, old people in nursing homes. The purpose is "to encourage people to be free and deep and extravagant in what they write so that they could find what was hidden in themselves that they had to say."

- To put the teachers in the mood for writing, it is often helpful to read some poems aloud. Here is a poem written by a seventh grader, who was inspired by Wallace Stevens' "Thirteen Ways of Looking at a Blackbird."

Five Ways of Looking at a Pond
—Molly Hankwitz, 7th Grade

A pond is just a mirror
    left alone, amongst the grasses
    to reflect the sky
A single tear from skies above
    finally cooled
    by evening winds
A shiny silver button
    dropped from a giant's coat
    never to be found
Made of green jade
    a Chinese bowl
    surrounded by leafy, green temples
Blue paint accidentally dribbled
    on the green carpet
    of a hill.

* In the excerpt below adapted from *Wishes, Lies and Dreams*, Koch describes some of the methods he uses with children. They would apply equally well to teachers interested in getting in touch with the poet in themselves. Read the following excerpt to the teachers, pausing to give them time to respond to each instruction in writing.

Think about your wishes, real wishes as wild and crazy as you like, and write a poem in which every line starts with "I wish … "

Look at some object in the room—your hand, a sheet of paper, a piece of chalk—and compare it to something which is like it in only one way. Write a comparison poem, using "like" or "as" in every line.

Write a poem that has a lie in every line or make up a whole poem in which nothing is true.

Think about how people often associate colors with sounds, places, words, numbers—then write a poem with a color in every line, the same color or different colors or different shades of the same color.

Think of differences between your past and present self and write a poem where you begin alternate lines with "I used to … "

and "But now … " or with "I used to be … " and "But now I am
… " or with "I used to think … " and "But now I know … "

* Have the teachers form cooperative groups, and read their poems
aloud to each other.

5. Role Playing

Objective: Teachers will learn to imagine and act out alternative forms of
behavior.

* Propose situations appropriate to the experience of the teachers, for
example:

   *A teacher is confronted by an angry parent regarding Christmas programs
   at school.*

   A teacher discovers another teacher is dating a student.

   A student asking for a change of grade from a teacher.

   Additional situations can be derived from the experiences of the teachers.

* Ask for volunteers to conduct a role-play; then have the teachers form
cooperative groups to brainstorm alternative role-plays.

* Have the volunteers repeat the role-play utilizing ideas formulated in
the brainstorming.

* Now have the groups brainstorm recent incidents that they wish had
turned out differently. After a situation is chosen, allow a few minutes
for volunteer players in each group to feel their way into their roles
and set the scene. Within the limits of the situation, encourage the
players to define the character as they wish.

* Have each group make use of alter egos: When someone in the group
thinks of an alternative response, she or he can come forward, put a
hand on the shoulder of the speaker and voice the alternative.

* Now have each group make use of role reversal: when the scene is fin-
ished, the person who played the parent takes the role of the teacher,
etc.

6. Life Planning
Adapted in part from George A. Ford
and Gordon Lippitt: *Planning Your Future.*

Note: This exercise requires a good deal of time—at least six to eight hours,
preferably divided into three or four sessions with several days in between,
so that teachers can approach each set of exercises with fresh energies.

Teachers should save the materials generated in the exercises, as each session builds upon materials produced earlier.

Objectives: (1) Teachers will be better able to envisage possible futures for themselves. (2) Teachers will develop skill in clarifying and prioritizing broad life goals.

- Have the teachers draw their life line on a sheet of paper, using the left edge of the paper to represent life's beginning and the right edge its end, and making a check mark to indicate where they are now.

- Now have the teachers form cooperative groups, share and discuss their drawings answering the following questions: *Why did you draw your line as you did? Where are the most significant turning points in your line? Where are the most important decisions that you made?*

- Ask each teacher to reflect and write down anything that they learned about her/himself.

- Distribute the following list and have the teachers identify personal life goals.

  affection—to obtain and share companionship and affection

  duty—to dedicate myself to what I call duty

  expertness—to become an authority in some field

  independence—to have freedom of thought and action

  leadership—to become influential

  parenthood—to raise a family, to have heirs

  pleasure—to enjoy life, to be happy and contented

  power—to have control of others

  prestige—to become well known

  security—to have a secure and stable position

  self-realization—to optimize my personal development

  service—to contribute to the welfare of others

  wealth—to earn a great deal of money

- Now have the teachers rank this list in terms of their own values from (1) for most important to (13) for least important. Have them do this quickly, in terms of first reactions; then go back and review, changing them if necessary.

Goals can vary, both in their clarity and in the degree of commitment we have toward them. Here is a four-point scale:

1. High clarity-high commitment. (I know where I want to go, and I am eager to get there).

2. High clarity-low commitment. (I know where I am supposed to go, but I do not want to).

3. Low clarity-high commitment. (I want to do something, but I am not sure what).

4. Low clarity-low commitment. (I do not feel like doing anything, and I do not care).

* Have the teachers review their five top priorities and evaluate them in terms of the above four-point scale.

* Have the teachers write down two or three small first steps they could take now to move toward their goals and have them discuss those steps in their group.

* Have the teachers write a brief biography and sketch out an ideal day or two in their lives in the relatively near future.

* Now have the teachers exchange statements with the members of their group. Have each teacher take the statements of one other and look for the goals that are explicit or implicit in them.

* Ask the teachers to think about their careers and write eight or ten statements of attainments they would like to achieve. Then have them do the same for relationships.

* Now have them rank each of the items on the above two lists according to the following four-point scale:

1. Not important.

2. Somewhat important.

3. Of great importance.

4. Of highest importance.

* Have each teacher make a list of the six items of highest importance and the six of least importance; then, have them share and discuss statements, rankings and priorities.

* Now have the teachers write down their responses to the following categories as quickly and spontaneously as they can. Overlaps and duplications do not matter.

1. Peak experiences I have had—great moments when I felt really alive.

2. Things I would like to learn to do well either because I must or because I want to.

3. Things I would like to stop doing—family, friends, co-workers might have suggestions.

4. Peak experiences I would like to have.

5.   Things I would like to start doing now (note these down just as they come to mind; don't censor anything).

*   Have the teachers share and discuss their responses with their group. Ask the teachers to compare their list of things they would like to do now with their five top priority life goals and with the six top items in who they would like to be.

*   Ask the teachers if they believe that their action steps are reasonably consistent with their goals? If the answer is no, tell them that they may want to reconsider and try to locate causes of the discrepancies.

*   Indicate to the teachers that they need not devise a separate plan for every goal they have in mind. Tell them to try to combine several goals into one concrete approach and to find others who share their goals and are willing to join with them.

*   Have the teachers review their highest priority items and write them down. Tell them to be sure to include:
    your three highest broad life goals
    your small first steps to action
    three long range goals from your autobiography
    the peak experiences you would like to have
    the things you would like to start doing now

*   By combining some of these goals, desires and actions, have the teachers write out at least three concrete plans for themselves.

EXERCISES TO DEVELOP SYSTEMS SKILLS FOR TEACHERS

Systems Skills: The ability to see the various parts of a system as they relate to the whole and to plan for systemic changes. These are the last to be developed because they depend on the development and integration of the other three sets of skills.

Systems Skills

1. Identifying the various systems at work in one's own life.
2. Identifying a system in terms of its component parts and their functions and interactions.
3. Distinguishing between process and content in group interaction.
4. Understanding the body as a system.
5. Acquiring sufficient knowledge of nutrition, exercise, relaxation techniques to choose those which are best suited to oneself.
6. Making a system analysis of one's family.
7. Defining one's own role in one's systems.
8. Ability to cope with bureaucratic paper work (attendance forms, registration forms, E.S.E. documentation).
9. Defining one's role in one's political grouping.
10. Assessing the strong and weak points of specific institutions.
11. Synthesizing data from a variety of sources (e.g., personal experience, statistics, interviews, research reports, emotional inputs, etc.).
12. Ability to make sense out of apparently disparate data.
13. Ability to organize a task, dividing it into its component parts.
14. Developing informal communication and support networks within a formal educational system.
15. Engaging in long-term planning and goal setting for oneself.
16. Engaging in long-term planning and goal setting for schools.
17. Communicating effectively with persons at different levels in a given system (e.g., fellow teachers, administrators, students).

Each day, teachers must deal with a large number of complex, highly abstract, bureaucratic systems which sustain schools and pattern teacher behavior.

The teacher who has System skills is not only able to follow the rules and regulations of the school system of which he or she is a part but also can exercise more advanced skills. He or she is able to think of the system as a whole, identify the parts, understand how these parts interrelate, and communicate those understandings. He or she is able to make judgments about the worth of the system and has the skill to intervene to make the necessary changes. Educators in leadership positions—those having responsibility for structuring an organization, developing policies and procedures (such as teachers on school improvement teams)—need well-developed Systems skills.

Systems skills require adequate development and integration of the other three sets of skills. Coping with the day-to-day problems of getting along in schools may require Instrumental skills, such as the ability to fill out the necessary forms or to locate the right person to call in an emergency. One may even employ Imaginal skills in figuring out how to take advantage of the system in small ways. For example, most teachers learn how to deal with the registration system to get the credits they need for recertification or a raise they want or how to deal with the office to secure a desirable classroom. But these coping skills do not qualify as full Systems skills as we are using the term.

Analyzing Existing Systems

1. Time Management

One basic method of improving the way in which we accomplish what we intend is to manage time. If we are constantly under pressure to complete tasks, as teachers often are, it leaves less energy for other areas of development. Teachers can therefore profit by a systematic approach to time management.

Objective: Teachers will develop skills in time management strategies.

 * Ask each teacher to select a task that they must complete by a certain date and list all the things that must be done (sub-tasks) before the task is completed.

    1.
    2.
    3.
    4.
    5.
    6.
    7.
    8.

9.
10.
11.
12.

* For each sub-task, have the teacher decide how long it will take and choose a date by which it must be completed.
* Distribute to each teacher a large calendar. *(See page opposite.)* Have them draw lines on the calendar to represent each sub-task and the time it will take to complete it. Instruct them to start first with those sub-tasks which have a firm starting or finishing date; then add others, taking care that they do not have too many things to do all at once. Point out that by creating a series of due dates, they have created an orderly system for getting the job done without going through the pressure and confusion of a last minute rush.
* Have the teachers review their schedule again, this time noting other possible time conflicts which might arise from school, family or other commitments or opportunities. Now ask them to shift task completion schedule as necessary.
* Have the teachers form cooperative groups and discuss their ideas and observations.

Example

Task: To write a school improvement plan which is due December 3. Assignment given September 15.

Sub-task list:

Meet with committee	Write first draft
Seek input from school community	Revise draft
Draft outline	Type plan
Receive Feedback	Proofread plan
Revise outline	Committee approves plan
Write Introduction	Submit plan December 3, 9 A.M.

2. Developing a Budget

Another starting point for building Systems skills is the development of the ability to handle money. Not only is this an important skill and an essential aspect of any school, but it is also a process which can be revealing with

SEPTEMBER

S	M	T	W	T	F	S
			1	2	3	4
5	6	7	8	9	10	11
12	13	14	15	16	17	18

CHOOSE →

19	20	21	22	23	24	25

TOPIC FOR PAPER → · RESOURCES →

26	27	28	29	30

DRAFT OUTLINE • RESEARCH TIME →

OCTOBER

S	M	T	W	T	F	S
					1	2

RESEARCH →

3	4	5	6	7	8	9

TIME — REVISE OUTLINE → SUBMIT OUTLINE →

10	11	12	13	14	15	16

RESEARCH TIME → WEEKEND GUESTS →

17	18	19	20	21	22	23

WRITE INTRODUCTION → WRITE FIRST DRAFT →

24	25	26	27	28	29	30

STUDY FOR MID-TERM EXAMS

31

NOVEMBER

S	M	T	W	T	F	S
	1	2	3	4	5	6

MID-TERM EXAMS WEEK   PARTY!

7	8	9	10	11	12	13

REVISE DRAFT →

14	15	16	17	18	19	20

OUT-OF-TOWN TRIP

21	22	23	24	25	26	27

OUT-OF-TOWN TRIP — PROOFREAD PAPER →

28	29	30

MAKE LAST

DECEMBER

S	M	T	W	T	F	S
			1	2	3	4

CHANGES →   SUBMIT PAPER

respect to value development. Decisions educators make about spending money are reflections of their choices about what is important.

Objective: Teachers will improve financial management skills.

- Have the teachers spend about ten minutes listing all the expenses they can remember having over the past few months. Tell them not to be concerned over the amount paid; just list the items. They might come up with such things as:

shoes	*gas*	*party supplies*	*tires*
rent	*theater tickets*	*insurance*	*school supplies*
club dues	*tuition*	*food*	*toothpaste*
haircut	*parking fees*	*dry cleaning*	*overdue book fines*

- Now have them decide which items are fixed and which are flexible. Fixed items are those for which periodic and prearranged payment is due, such as rent and tuition. Flexible items are those which you buy from time to time and over which you have more control in terms of when you will buy them and what they will cost. Instruct them to circle those which are fixed.

- Based on their recall of their main items of expense, they are now prepared to make a budget projection for the coming month or months. Ask them to develop a worksheet such as the one on the previous page, adjusting it for their situation.

- In order to improve their ability to predict expenses, you might have them construct a ledger which keeps track of their daily expenses. Or

DAILY EXPENSE RECORD

Income for month
$_____

Cash on hand first day of
month $_____

Month of _____

EXPENSES	1	2	3	4	5	6	7	8	9	10
1. Food										
2. Rent										
3. Utilities										
4. Etc.										

better yet, use accounting software such as Quicken to develop monthly or quarterly summaries. With a clear idea of their existing spending patterns, they should be able to make better decisions about setting priorities based on their income and goals.

3. Awareness of Systems

Improving Systems skills depends on the ability to analyze the systems in which an individual is participating. Any system is a complex whole with interacting parts, each of which may be studied as a separate sub-system or as a set of interrelationships. As a first step, it is useful for teachers to be aware of the many systems of which they are a part.

Objective: Teachers will become more aware of the various systems in which they are now functioning.

- Have the teachers list at least ten systems in which they are now participating along with their particular role in each. To help generate ideas, ask them to trace a path through daily activities or look inside their wallet or purse.

SYSTEM	ROLE
1. School system	1. Teacher
2. Family	2. Parent
3.	
4.	
5.	
6.	
7.	
8.	
9.	
10.	

- Have them check their system list against the following list of systems:

SYSTEM	ROLE
Business	Customer
School	Teacher
Political System	Voter, office-holder, taxpayer
Police Department	Consumer of service

Hospital	Patient
Team	Member
Church	Member of congregation
Club	Office holder
Committee	Member
Armed Forces	Private
Legal System	Contract signer, defendant
Insurance	Payer of premiums
Utilities	Consumer
Banking System	Borrower, saver
Credit Card System	User
Television	Viewer
Library	Borrower
Your Body	Manager
Ecological System	Nourisher or Destroyer

4. System Analysis

Objective: Teachers will be better able to identify the various parts of a given system.

- Ask each teacher to select one of the systems identified in the previous exercise and list all the parts they can think of.

Example

System: Bus System

Parts: Bus driver, roads, routing schedule, repair service, gas or electricity sources, manufacturer, advertisers, designer of interior, insurance, technical designer, legal department, company management, payroll, transportation as a service value, safety, fare rates.

- Now have the teachers arrange the elements of this system under the following categories:
  1. Purposes, aims, functions
  2. Basic resources used
  3. Technology (machinery/skills)
  4. Personnel (Who does the work?)
  5. Finance (How does the system get started? keep going?)
  6. Legal aspects
  7. Management structure (organizational chart)
  8. Aesthetic considerations

9. Health and environmental considerations

❧ Have the teachers form small groups and as a group repeat the exercise for the "school" system.

❧ Ask the groups to discuss the following questions: *Do you have any elements in any of your systems that do not fit the nine categories? Were there any categories without system parts?*

Developing Vision About Systems Change

How do we improve the school environment? How do we make our schools work better for everyone involved—teachers, students, administrators, staff, parents, community? A first step requires a vision, an idea of what we would like to see happen. We need to make value judgments about what is good, about the direction of change we want to encourage and work toward. We assume that teachers will be happier, more productive and fulfilled, when they are functioning with a vision of what direction they want for themselves and for others. The following exercises will illustrate ways of applying a value-based vision to systems.

1. Your Classroom as a System: Physical Space

Physical space embodies values. Fixed seats facing a teacher's desk on a raised platform are a physical expression of a hierarchy. This format is a way of stating that the only, or the most important, source of knowledge in the room is behind the desk. Seating in a circle or around a table is a physical expression of equality; it is a way of indicating that everyone has something to say that is worth listening to.

Objectives: (1) Teachers will envision an ideal physical set-up. (2) Teachers will identify the values embodied in the physical set-up.

1. Each teacher makes a list of the major features she/he would like in an ideal classroom: size, lighting, temperature, equipment, etc.
2. Each one rank orders the list, starting with (1) for the most important single feature.
3. Form small groups—four or five people—to share lists.
4. Groups attempt to arrive at a single model.
5. Groups then identify the values embodied in the various features of their model.
6. If time allows, groups share their work with each other.

2. Your Classroom as a System: Social Space and Inclusion

Your classroom is a microcosm of society. In any group there will be an amazing diversity of physical types, temperaments, abilities, experiences, values. Moreover, these diverse individuals form ever shifting alliances, pairings, cliques, based on mutual likes and dislikes. Teachers ignore these dynamics at their peril. The dynamics are a given—the question is how to use them creatively to support, rather than hamper, the learning process. The objective is not to maintain control for the sake of a smoothly functioning classroom, but rather to create an environment that will nurture human growth. As we have said above, the majority of your students probably will be in Phase II, although in nursery school and the early elementary grades many are likely to be in Phase I. This means that the teacher who is concerned for value development must reinforce the basic values of Phases I and II, namely, Safety and Security, Acceptance and Belonging, while at the same time providing concrete examples of Phase III values, such as Creativity and Independence. When an individual enjoys the security of Belonging and being accepted, it is easier to take the risks involved in Creativity.

The following exercise on the dynamics of inclusion suggests ways in which to reinforce Acceptance and Belonging in the classroom.

Objective: Teachers will become acquainted with methods for assuring inclusion in the classroom.

1. Each teacher takes ten minutes to reflect on his/her experiences in this course, looking for examples of inclusion or exclusion.
2. Discuss in small groups what methods were used to assure inclusion of all members of the total group or sub-groups, e.g., arrangement of physical space, provision of materials for all participants, setting an initial task that requires every group member to speak, etc.
3. Discuss how teachers can apply these methods in the classroom.
4. How can teachers deal with the shy or introverted individual who tends to remain silent? the need to respect the individual's privacy and right to choose? the legitimation of "I pass" as a response? Cf. the example in Montessori schools; on the one hand, the circle in which all are expected to participate; on the other hand, the privacy mats that signal the desire of the individual to be undisturbed.

3. Creating Social Space: The Cooperative Squares Exercise
To reinforce the Phase II value of Belonging, it is important to create a collaborative and supportive environment rather than a competitive one.
Objectives: (1) Teachers will identify elements basic to creating a cooperative environment. (2) Teachers will test these elements experientially.

1. Divide participants into groups of six.
2. Each group discusses and makes a list of the elements that are essential for a group to cooperate on a task, e.g., everyone must understand the task, each one must recognize and be supportive of the contributions of others, no put-downs, each one must be willing to make his/her maximum contribution, each must be willing to aid the others in making their maximum contribution, etc.
3. The groups choose one of their number to act as observer. The facilitator gives this person the instructions for the observer.
4. The facilitator distributes each group's packet of envelopes and the instructions to each group. The instructions are read aloud and all questions answered before the signal to begin is given.
5. After all the groups have completed the task, they discuss the experience, focussing first on their own feelings as participants, then soliciting observations from the observer and finally relating insights from this experience to building cooperation in the classroom.

Instructions for the Group
This packet contains five envelopes, each of which holds several pieces of cardboard for forming squares. When the signal is given, the task for your group is to form five squares of equal size. The task is not completed until each individual has before him/her a perfect square the same size as that held by others. The following rules are to be observed during this exercise:

*   No member may speak.
*   No member may ask another member for a piece or in any way signal that another is to give her/him a piece.
*   Members may, however, give pieces to other members.

Instructions for the Observer
Your job is to do your best to enforce the rules.

*   No talking, pointing, or any other kind of communicating among the members.

- Members may give pieces to others but may not take pieces from others.
- Members may not throw their pieces into the center for others to take; they must give pieces directly to one individual.
- Members may give away all the pieces to their puzzle, even after already having formed a square.

As observer, you may want to look for some of the following:

- Who is willing to give away pieces of the puzzle?
- Did anyone finish the puzzle and then sit back, divorced from the struggles of the group?
- Do some struggle with their pieces but are unwilling to give any away?
- Periodically check the level of frustration and anxiety.
- Was there a critical turning point when the group began to cooperate?
- Did anyone try to violate the rules by talking or pointing?

Directions for Making a Set of Squares

A packet consists of five envelopes containing pieces of cardboard cut according to the pattern below, which, when properly arranged, will form five squares of equal size. Cut out five cardboard squares, each 6" by 6", mark them as below, and cut out the pieces.

Mark the envelopes A, B, C, D, E and distribute the pieces as follows:

A: i, h, e

B: a, a, a, c

C: a, j

D: d, f

E: g, b, f, c

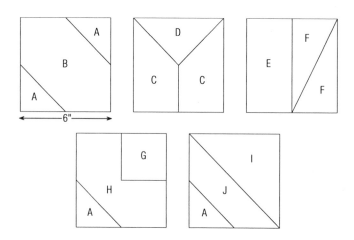

Erase the pencilled letter from each piece and write instead the appropriate envelope letter to facilitate return of the pieces to the proper envelope when the group has completed its task.

4. Your Classroom as a System: Authority Relations

Authority relations are a critical element in the dynamics of any social space. Teachers, along with parents, are usually the most important authority figures many young people meet in their early years and therefore play a major role in forming students' attitudes toward authority.

Objective: Teachers will analyze authority relations in classroom systems.

- Distribute classroom organization charts and divide teachers into two groups.
- Ask one group to discuss each item and decide which system they would choose in an ideal school.
- Ask the other group to review each item and decide which system reflects the present reality of their school.
- Ask the two groups to compare their responses and analyze the causes of any differences.
- Form two new groups, each made up of half of group I and half of group II. Ask them to develop plans to move the real school toward the ideal.

NOTE: *Cooperative learning* is a powerful way of creating a supportive environment, enabling the teacher to tap into the energies of the group to promote, rather than impede, learning.

See *Circles of Learning* by David and Roger Johnson and Edythe Holubec for ways of structuring learning groups to promote interdependence in goals, roles, resources, tasks, products. These methods produce a sense of "we are all in this together, sink or swim." Cooperative learning promotes liking, acceptance and mutual helpfulness among students as well as increased achievement for all participants

Cooperative discipline is another crucial dynamic in the classroom. See Linda Albert, *Cooperative Discipline,* and Dinkmeyer et al, *Systematic Training for Effective Teaching,* both published by American Guidance Services, for further material on this topic.

Relating to Larger Systems

Your classroom is a part of larger systems extending outward in concentric circles of mutual influence, opportunity and constraint. For example, political decisions on school financing at the state and even national level will impact your classroom as surely as the more immediate decision of an administrator to interrupt student learning with announcements over the intercom. As teachers, it is helpful for you to identify those system "actors and factors" which you and your colleagues might seek to utilize or influence when you draw up plans for student learning.

1. Your Classroom Within Larger Systems

Objective: To identify the various actors and factors which form the system in which your classroom operates.

Resources: Overhead projector or newsprint

- Write ACTORS AND FACTORS at the top of a transparency or newsprint sheet.
- Take two or three minutes for each person to list, on individual sheets of paper, five social forces, people, policies, or practices that have an impact on the classroom.
- Then form groups of four or five and develop a list of at least 12 forces.
- Use the overhead projector or newsprint to develop a common list.
- The group should then consider each actor or factor as a potential asset or constraint to the education mission.
- As a separate exercise, make judgments about what values are implicit in your discussion of the ways these system elements impact teaching and learning.

2. Dealing with Authority

There is a certain gentle art teachers must learn in dealing with human systems so that they work for them and not against them. Businesses, for example, are supposed to provide services and products at reasonable costs. But what if a consumer is overcharged or receives shoddy merchandise? What should a teacher do if, at school, the principal keeps asking him/her to do extra work as a personal favor but he or she does not offer any additional pay?

Many teachers have turned to "assertiveness" as a technique which allows them to own power as a person.

FOUR TYPES OF CLASSROOM ORGANIZATION

	A	B	C	D
How much confidence is shown in individual students in the classroom?	Very little	Some	Substantial	A great deal
How free do students feels to talk to the teacher?	Not very free	Somewhat free	Rather free	Very free
Is predominant use made of 1. fear, 2. threats, 3. punishments, 4. rewards, 5. involvement to control students in the classroom?	1, 2, 3, occasionally 4	4, some 3	4, some 3 and 5	5, 4 based on group-set goals
How candid is communication between teachers and students?	Very cautious	Quite cautious	Often candid	Usually candid
What is the basis for decision making?	School policy exclusively	School policy and teacher judgement	School policy, teacher judgement, some student consideration	By teacher and students within school policy
Are students involved in decisions related to their clasroom obligations?	Not very often	Occasionally consulted	Generally consulted	Fully involved
How are classroom organizational goals established?	Directions given by teacher	Teacher direction, some opportunity for comments by students	After discussion, teacher decides	By group decision as a rule
How is classroom performance reviewed and evaluated?	Almost always by teacher alone	Teacher listens to student, but makes evaluation alone	Evaluation somewhat shared by teacher	Evaluation widely shared by teacher and student
What are test scores and other control data used for?	Keep student in line, punish for failure	Keep student in line, reward and punishment	Control through reward and self-guidance	Largely for self-direction and problem solving

Being assertive is the art of conducting yourself in such a way that you are neither a passive doormat, denying your own rights (non-assertive), nor a ranting, obnoxious person who tramples on the rights of others (aggressive).

Objective: Teachers will be able to recognize the difference between non-assertive, assertive, and aggressive behavior.

* Ask the teachers to assume they have been overcharged on their tuition

fee for graduate education courses. They had dropped a course, but are still being billed as if they continued in the course, and they are sure they were within the time limit allowed for cancellation. Below are some possible responses they might make.

* Have the teachers form cooperative groups and review the following behaviors.

* Ask them to determine whether the behavior is non-assertive behavior, assertive behavior or aggressive behavior.

1. Call home and tell your family about the tyranny of the college bursar.
2. Call your lawyer and prepare for a lawsuit.
3. Demand that the clerk in the bursar's office fix the error immediately or you will go directly to the president with the case.
4. Go to the president's office and complain about the gross inefficiency of the bursar's office.
5. Call for an appointment to see the bursar and present your problem.
6. Write a letter to the bursar in which you include xeroxed copies of relevant transactions and ask that you receive a new bill.
7. Send off a quick note to the university academic accrediting agency about your case with a copy to the bursar to insure quick action.
8. Wait for a while to see if the college corrects its mistake.

* Groups which designated responses 1 and 8 as non-assertive, 5 and 6 as assertive, and 2, 3, 4, and 7 as aggressive, are correct. Point out that response 1 is misdirected energy and is an avoidance behavior and that aggressive responses either impose unnecessarily on others' time or threaten other people without justification. Such behavior creates enemies very rapidly!

* Have the groups brainstorm other assertive approaches they might use in this situation.

3. Applying Assertiveness

Remember that assertiveness involves at the outset a change of attitude about oneself as a person. As human beings, teachers have a basic set of rights and responsibilities with respect to others. In American culture, they include:

1. Command over your time, your property and your body.
2. The right to express your opinion; to express yourself.

3. The right to be respected as a person.
4. The right to refuse a request.
5. The right to ask for things that you need.
6. The right to question those in authority.
7. The right to be angry with others
8. The right to be wrong on occasion.
9. The right to not have to justify every action to others.
10. The right to be less than perfect in your work.
11. The right to not be liked by everyone.

Objective: Teachers will gain skills in assertive behavior.

- Have the teachers describe in writing a situation in which they did not act with assertiveness or a situation that is coming up soon in which assertiveness would be useful.
- Have them form cooperative groups and have the groups designate an observer.
- Ask two in each group to role play the situation. The observer should keep track of non-assertive, assertive and aggressive elements.
- Have the groups discuss the role play; change roles and repeat.

Many teachers become afraid when faced with authority figures. It is useful therefore to distinguish between rational anxiety, rationalization and irrational thought. "What if he fires me?" and "It probably won't do any good anyway" are examples of irrational thinking and rationalization. Teachers should try to face a situation realistically and make some rational judgments about what will be the probable effect of acting assertively. Usually, an assertive person will, by his or her behavior, produce a favorable reaction from others simply because his or her behavior is viewed as appropriate and legitimate.

4. Identifying Group Values

Teachers belong to one or more groups, be they professional, social or community based. Each group represents, whether stated or not, a set of values. Groups, moreover, often are regarded by others as having certain value positions or standing for something of value. For example, the medical profession is associated with the value of health even though a given doctor many not be motivated by such high ideals all the time. Some groups may be quite aware of their value positions and make explicit statements, using codes of ethics, objectives and purposes, preambles to constitutions and the like.

Objective: Teachers will recognize that values are operative within an organized group.

- Have the teachers choose a specific group to which several now belong.
- Now have them form cooperative groups and write three or four reasons for the existence of the chosen groups in the first place.
- Give the teachers an extended period of time to collect and examine any formal statements of ethics or purpose that the chosen groups have produced.
- Now have them discuss at least five recent activities by the group.
- Have each small group carefully review the list of 125 values. (Found in the back of this book).
- Have them identify which of the values are operating within the group as expressed in group activities.

SECTION III

Appendices

Teacher's Journal

A Guide to the Role of Values in One's Daily Schedule

LARRY S. ROSEN
BRIAN P. HALL

TEACHER'S JOURNAL

THE PURPOSE OF the Teacher's Journal is to enable you as a teacher to become aware of how you use time and what values are implicit in that use.

Daily Time Report

The following forms will provide an opportunity to categorize how your time is used during each 24-hour period for one week. Begin by listing all significant activities in the column entitled "Activity." A significant activity is one that takes a half hour or more of your time or has a great impact on you. An example of a significant activity that might not take a half hour but has a great impact on you would be a 5-minute telephone call from an old friend you haven't spoken to for three years.

In the column entitled "W/Person," indicate who shared each activity with you. Some activities will be done on your own, in which case you should indicate "self." Other activities will be shared with one to three people, in which case you should list their names. If the activity is shared with more than three people, describe the nature of the group, such as family, neighbors, colleagues, etc. It is important to understand that an activity is only shared if you are somehow interacting with another person. In cases where people may be in the room with you but are not interacting with you, that time should be considered time with "self." An example of this would be watching television with another person in the room. Interaction, however, need not be verbal. If you are watching television with a person and are consistently conscious of their presence, this activity would be one that is shared.

It is important to keep track of all of your daily activities, together with the individuals or groups with whom time was spent, for at least one week.

Categories of Time:

In the upper right hand corner of your Daily Time Report is a section entitled "Categories of Time." The purpose of this section is to enable you to identify how much time you spend in each of five categories. In some cases, it will be difficult to determine which category is most appropriate. When this occurs, just divide the time between the categories that apply. At the end of each day, this section should always add up to 24 hours. It is useful, however, to round time out to the nearest half hour. Review carefully the following categories to determine how to distribute time in this section.

Work

Work occurs during a limited number of hours, at a specific place, for a specific purpose. Work time includes any time you are doing something related to your role as a teacher or for which you receive payment. It also includes time spent on activities directly related to being a graduate student in any academic or technical setting. Time spent as a volunteer where there is a clear commitment or contract to an organization is also considered work time. The key to identifying work time is the understanding that it is time where you are concerned with duty, obligation and the expectations of others.

Maintenance

Maintenance time can be best described as resting, recuperating and upkeep. This time includes the time spent meeting the needs of others outside a school setting. As such, it may be the most psychologically draining of all the categories. It is time you are concerned with recuperating from work, maintaining the physical and emotional well-being of yourself and others, and maintaining your property. Maintenance time is also that time that enables you to work. Some examples of maintenance time would be traveling to and from work, going to the doctor, listening to a friend's problems, sharing your problems with a friend, mowing the grass and putting your feet up and relaxing after a long day. In many cases, maintenance time overlaps work or play time. Although sleep may be a form of maintenance, it should always be considered separately for the purposes of this journal.

Play

Play time is time that does not involve duty or obligation. Play may occur at planned times or may be spontaneous. It involves fantasizing, searching and celebrating. Play time is always fun. If it isn't fun … it's not play! We only play with people we like. For example, if you go to a party with your spouse's friends whom you don't particularly like, that time would be maintenance time rather than play time because it isn't really enjoyable for you; but you are there maintaining your relationship with your spouse and helping to maintain your spouse's relationships with others. Play time occurs when you spend time with people you enjoy and with whom you have a lot of fun. It is possible to play by yourself, but play time usually involves others. Play requires trustful relationships and may include occasional excess.

Freesence

Freesence occurs at a high level of consciousness. It involves being with and contemplation of the environment. During freesence, time becomes unlimited, a moment may seem like an hour or an hour like a moment. One becomes totally a part of one's environment and experiences at-one-ness with the surroundings. Freesence involves being, waiting and seeing. Whether alone or with another person, one experiences intimacy and unity.

Freesence involves activities that move toward intimacy or solitude. Time is unprogrammed, but regularly allotted for. Examples might include reading poetry, sexual intimacy, looking at a work of art, a walk in the woods during which you feel at one with nature, or a deeply meaningful spiritual or religious experience. Freesence is celebration, festivity and meaning.

Sleep

Sleep means that you are asleep. This includes time dreaming and napping. It may be that you sleep with someone, but during actual sleep you are alone. You may wish to record your dreams in the "feelings" section of your journal. Sleep is usually considered a form of maintenance, but for the purpose of this journal we are considering it separately.

Daily Feelings

In this section, record the experiences you had during the day that were especially significant. These experiences may be positive or negative. Identify the feelings these experiences generated within you. You may wish to refer to Rosenberg's list of "Feeling Words." Discuss problems you are dealing with and brainstorm solutions. You need to write at least one hundred words to help you reflect upon your day.

Example

Record feelings, decisions and behaviors you experienced or acted upon today.

> I had a difficult time with Andy and his parents today and am feeling disheartened. Andy is sleeping in class and still hurting other students. His parents don't seem to care, which irritates me. I'm feeling frustrated that I can't seem to get through to them.
> On the other hand, I'm thrilled that Ryan and Zenta won the state science contest. I was confident Ryan would win and feel pleased and proud. Zenta was a big surprise and I feel overjoyed.
> Things are going better in my relationship with Tom. He has become more open and seems willing to consider team teaching. I feel better, but still apprehensive.

PLEASE NOTE: Be open and honest with yourself. If you intend to share this journal with others, plan to mark out with a black marker those sections that are too personal to share. This will enable you to be completely open with yourself and yet ensure your privacy.

Time and Your Values

Each day, carefully read the list of 125 Values (at the end of this book) and their definitions. Some of the values will be clear and obvious to you, others may seem obscure. If you do not clearly understand the definition of a value, please look it up in a dictionary and discuss it with others.

As you read through the list, reflect on how you spent your time during the day, think about which of the values had an impact on how you chose to spend your time and which values motivated you, empowered you or resulted in arousing strong feelings in you.

Make seven copies of the form on the next page to record your daily feelings, decisions and behaviors and the values that had the greatest impact.

DAILY FEELINGS, DECISIONS AND BEHAVIORS

DAILY VALUES
List the five values that had the most impact on you and your day.

1.

2.

3.

4.

5.

ANALYZING VALUES

Review the values section on each of your forms. List all the values you have identified. Add up the number of times each value is chosen. In the spaces below, complete the list of the values chosen.

VALUE	TIMES CHOSEN	VALUE	TIMES CHOSEN

In writing, reflect upon the following:
* Are you spending sufficient time in the areas necessary to contribute to the development of your most frequently identified values?

* Do you have a plan to develop skills related to your most frequently identified values?

Developing a Personal Growth Plan

Reflect upon the definitions of your most frequently identified Values. Using language from the 125 Value definitions, write two Goal Statements for yourself.

Example: Service, Family and Competence. *I will develop the realistic and objective confidence that I have the teaching skills to make a contribution to my students and their families and to become more motivated to use those skills.*

Example: Honesty. *I will be better able to express my feelings and thoughts in a straightforward, objective manner.*

Goal Statements

1.

2.

The statements you have just written can become part of a Personal Growth Plan and can promote your development toward accomplishing your goals. You may wish to identify other frequently chosen Values to help you further develop a Personal Growth Plan.

Analysis of the Teacher's Journal

Complete the following calculations which will enable you to determine how much time was spent in each of the five categories and the percentage of time spent in each category as recorded in your Teacher's Journal.

- ✸ Calculate the number of hours spent during the week in each of the following categories: Work, Play, Maintenance, Freesence and Sleep.
- ✸ Figure the percentage of time spent in each category by dividing the number of hours in each by the total number of hours in the week (168 hours).

CATEGORY	TOTAL HOURS	% OF TOTAL TIME (DIVIDE BY 168)
WORK		
MAINTENANCE		
PLAY		
FREESENCE		
SLEEP		

The way you spent your time indicates where your priority values are and what your priority relationships are. For example, little time spent in Play or Freesence indicates a limited ability to be intimate with others or a heavy maintenance schedule and would indicate values such as Care or Service as opposed to Creativity and Intimacy.

The purpose of the following reflection questions and their interpretation is not to judge, but rather to help you to clarify how to use your time more effectively. Answer them in writing and then discuss with someone you trust.

- Am I satisfied with my overall use of time or do I wish to make some changes?

If you wish to make some changes, make them slowly and carefully. A change in one category of time will alter all the others.

If a change in work time is desired, make sure it is not really a question of inadequate maintenance time or skills.

An excessive amount of maintenance time (1½ times your work time or greater) may reflect inadequate interpersonal skills. Excessive emotional maintenance of others may result in neglecting one's own needs or increased dependency.

* Am I experiencing conflict between my home and my work (school) life? Explain.

Working long hours at school may indicate avoidance of close relationships with family or friends. Intimacy is essential to personal development. If it is lacking, you may need to reflect on the quality of your relationships.

If maintenance related to teaching is high, tension may result since family members may not be receiving adequate attention.

When two people in a relationship have high maintenance, tension is bound to result unless careful planning is given to the areas of Play or Freesence.

* Does my work time exceed 60 hours per week? (35% of total time)

A good definition of a workaholic is one whose work hours are greater than 60 per week. If this is the case, rigorous attention should be given to Play and physical exercise. This is particularly true if maintenance time is primarily emotional.

Workaholics experience increased stress in their lives, and, without adequate skills, this may lead to substance abuse or eating or sleeping disorders.

* Do I have any Freesence time? How has Freesence time added meaning to my life? Explain.

Freesence is a quality that emerges only beyond Play. Absence of Freesence may require attention to close and intimate friendships outside of school-related responsibilities. Also helpful would be hobbies or spiritual experiences that provide one's life with meaning.

Values Definitions

PHASES I, II, III, IV. SKILLS 1: Instrumental; 2: Interpersonal; 3: Imaginal; 4: Systems.

1. **accountability/ethics** The ability that flows from one's personal awareness of one's own system of moral principles to enrich others by addressing their conduct in relationship to their value system. This assumes the capacity to understand another's level of ethical maturity. *III, 4*

2. **achievement/success** Accomplishing something noteworthy and admirable in the world of work or education. *II, 1*

3. **adaptability/flexibility** To adjust one's self readily to changing conditions and to remain pliable during ongoing processes. *III, 2*

4. **administration/control** Having the authority to be in command, to exercise specific management functions and tasks in a business or institution, e.g. financial control, production planning, etc. *II, 1*

5. **affection/physical** Physical touching which expresses fondness or devotion. *I, 2*

6. **art/beauty** Experiencing and/or providing intense pleasure through that which is aesthetically appealing in both natural and person-made creations simply for the mental and emotional stimulation and the pleasure it provides. *III, 3*

7. **authority/honesty** The freedom to experience and express one's full range of feelings and thoughts in a straightforward, objective manner. This ability comes from a personal integration of thoughts and feelings and results in experiencing one's own integrity and power. *III, 2*

8. **being liked** To experience friendly feelings from one's peers. *II, 2*

9. **being self** The capacity to own one's truth about one's self and the world with objective awareness of personal strengths and limitations plus the ability to act both independently and cooperatively when appropriate. *III, 4*

10. **belief/philosophy** Adherence to a belief system, set of principles, or established philosophy that is based on universally accepted authoritative documents such as the Bible, Koran, or Upanishads, which espouse the concept of reverence for the universal order. *II, 1*

11. **care/nurture** To be physically and emotionally supported by family and friends throughout one's life from childhood through old age and to value doing the same for others. *II, 2*

12. **collaboration** The ability of an organizational Leader to cooperate interdependently with all levels of management to insure full and appropriate delegation of responsibility. *III, 4*

13. **communication/information** Effective and efficient transmission and flow of ideas and factual data within and between persons, departments and divisions of an organization. *II, 1*

14. **community/personalist** Sufficient depth and quality of commitment to a group, its members and its purpose so that both independent creativity and interdependent cooperation are maximized simultaneously. *IV, 2*

15. **community/supportive** The recognition and will to create a group of peers for the purpose of ongoing mutual support and creative enhancement of each individual. The additional awareness of the need for such a group in the work environment and with peer professionals, to enable one to detach from external pressures that deter one from acting with clarity on chosen values and ethical principles that might be otherwise compromised. *III, 2*

16. **competence/confidence** Realistic and objective confidence that one has the skill to achieve in the world of work and to feel that those skills are a positive contribution. *II, 1*

17. **competition** To be energized by a sense of rivalry, to be first or most respected in a given arena, e.g., sports, education or work. *II, 1*

18. **complementarity** The capacity to enable persons in a corporation or institution to work cooperatively with one another such that the unique skills and qualities of one individual supplement, support and enhance the skills and qualities of the others in the group. *III, 4*

19. **congruence** The capacity to experience and express one's feelings and thoughts in such a way that what one experiences internally and communicates externally to others is the same. *III, 2*

20. **construction/new order** To develop and initiate a new institution for the purpose of creatively enhancing society. This assumes technological, interpersonal and management skills. *III, 4*

21. **contemplation** Self-discipline and the art of meditative prayer that prepares one for intimacy with others and unity with the universal order. *III, 3*

22. **control/order/discipline** Providing restraint and direction to achieve methodological arrangements of persons or things according to the prescribed rules. *II, 1*

23. **convivial technology** The capacity to creatively apply technological expertise, both organizationally and with technical instruments, to develop means to improve social conditions in the world by improving means of distributing the basic necessities of life. *IV, 4*

24. **corporation/new order** The skills, capacity and will to create new organizational styles or to improve present institutional forms in order to creatively enhance society. *III, 4*

25. **courtesy/hospitality** Offering polite and respectful treatment to others as well as treating guests and strangers in a friendly and generous manner. It also includes receiving the same treatment from others. *II, 2*

26. **creativity** The capacity for original thought and expression that brings new ideas and images into a practical and concrete reality in ways that did not previously exist. *III, 3*

27. **decision/initiation** To feel that it is one's responsibility to begin a creative course of action, or to act on one's conscience without external prompting. *III, 2*

28. **design/pattern/order** Awareness of the natural arrangement of things plus the ability to create new arrangements through the initiation of arts, ideas or technology, e.g. architecture. *II, 3*

29. **detachment/solitude** The regular discipline of non-attachment that leads to quality relationships with others and the universal order. *III, 3*

30. **dexterity/coordination** Sufficient harmonious interaction of mental and physical functions to perform basic instrumental skills. *II, 1*

31. **discernment** The capacity or skill to enable a group or organization to come to consensus decisions relative to long term planning through openness, reflection and honest interaction. *III, 4*

32. **duty/obligation** Closely following established customs and regulations out of dedication to one's peers and a sense of responsibility to institutional codes. *II, 2*

33. **economics/profit** Accumulation of physical wealth to be secure and respected. *I, 1*

34. **economics/success** To attain favorable and prosperous financial results in business through effective control and efficient management of resources. *II, 1*

35. **ecority** The capacity, skills and personal, organizational or conceptual influence to enable persons to take authority for the created order of the world and to enhance its beauty and balance through creative technology in ways that have worldwide influence. *IV, 4*

36. **education/certification** Completing a formally prescribed process of learning and receiving documentation of that process. *II, 1*

37. **education/knowledge** The experience of ongoing learning as a means of gaining new facts, truths and principles. One is motivated by the occasional reward of new understanding that is gained intuitively. *III, 3*

38. **efficiency/planning** Thinking about and designing acts and purposes in the best possible and least wasteful manner before implementing them. *II, 1*

39. **empathy** Reflecting and experiencing another's feelings and state of being through a quality of presence that has the consequence of seeing themselves with more clarity, without any words necessarily having been spoken. *III, 2*

40. **endurance/patience** The ability to bear difficult and painful experiences, situations or persons with calm stability and perseverance. *II, 2*

41. **equality/liberation** Experiencing one's self as having the same value and rights as all other human beings in such a way that one is set free to be that self and to free others to be themselves. This is the critical consciousness of the value of being human. *III, 2*

42. **equilibrium** Maintaining a peaceful social environment by averting upsets and avoiding conflicts. *II, 4*

43. **equity/rights** Awareness of the moral and ethical claim of all persons, including one's self, to legal, social and economic equality and fairness, plus a personal commitment to defend this claim. *III, 2*

44. **expressiveness/joy** To share one's feelings and fantasies so openly and spontaneously that others are free to do the same. *III, 3*

45. **faith/risk/vision** Behavioral commitment to values that are considered life-giving even at risk to one's life. *III, 3*

46. **family/belonging** The people to whom one feels primary bonds of relationship and acceptance and the place of dwelling of one's parents. *II, 2*

47. **fantasy/play** The experience of personal worth through unrestrained imagination and personal amusement. *II, 3*

48. **food/warmth/shelter** Personal concern about having adequate physical nourishment, warmth and comfort and a place of refuge from the elements. *I, 1*

49. **friendship/belonging** To have a group of persons with whom one can share on a day-to-day basis. *II, 2*

50. **function/physical** Concern about the ability to perform minimal manipulations of the body to care for one's self and concern about the body's internal systems and their ability to function adequately. *I, 1*

51. **generosity/compassion** Awareness of others' needs and limitations that leads to sharing one's unique gifts and skills as a way of serving others without expecting reciprocation. *III, 2*

52. **global harmony** Knowing the practical relationship between human oppression, freedom and creative ecological balance so that one can influence changes that promote the interdependence of peoples and nations, equality and creativity. *IV, 4*

53. **global justice** Commitment to the fact that all persons have equal value but different

gifts and abilities to contribute to society, combined with the capacity to elicit inter-institutional and governmental collaboration that will help provide the basic life necessities for the poor or disadvantaged in the world. *IV, 4*

54. **growth/expansion** The ability to enable an organization to develop and grow creatively. This assumes skills in management design, organizational, product and market development at a division or corporate level. *III, 4*

55. **health/healing** Soundness of mind and body that flows from meeting one's emotional and physical needs through self-awareness and preventive discipline. This includes an understanding that commitment to maintaining one's inner rhythm and balance relates to positive feelings and fantasy. *III, 4*

56. **hierarchy/order** The methodical, harmonious arrangement of persons and things ranked above one another in conformity to established standards of what is good and proper within an organization. *II, 4*

57. **honor** High respect for the worth, merit or rank of those in authority, e.g., parents, superiors and national leaders. *II, 4*

58. **human dignity** Consciousness of the basic right of every human being to have respect and to have his/her needs met that will allow him/her the opportunity to develop his/her potential. *III, 4*

59. **human rights** Committing one's talent, education, training and resources to creating the means for every person in the world to experience his/her basic right to such life-giving resources as food, habitat, employment, health and minimal practical education. *IV, 4*

60. **independence** Thinking and acting for one's self in matters of opinion, conduct, etc., without being subject to external constraint or authority. *III, 3*

61. **integration/wholeness** The inner capacity to organize the personality (mind and body) into a coordinated, harmonious totality. *III, 4*

62. **interdependence** Seeing and acting on the awareness that personal and inter-institutional cooperation are always preferable to individual decision-making. *IV, 4*

63. **intimacy** Sharing one's full personhood (thoughts, feelings, fantasies and realities) mutually and freely with the total personhood of another on a regular basis. *III, 2*

64. **intimacy/solitude** Experience of personal harmony that results from a combination of meditative practice, mutual openness and total acceptance of another person which leads to new levels of meaning and awareness of truth in unity with the universal order. *IV, 2*

65. **justice/social order** Taking a course of action that addresses, confronts and helps correct conditions of human oppression in order to actualize the truth that every human being is of equal value. *III, 4*

66. **knowledge/insight** The pursuit of truth through patterned investigation. One is

motivated by increased intuition and unconsciously-gained understanding of the wholeness of reality. *III, 4*

67. **law/guide** Seeing authoritative principles and regulations as a means for creating one's own criteria and moral conscience, and questioning those rules until they are clear and meaningful. *III, 4*

68. **law/rule** Governing one's conduct, action and procedures by the established legal system or code. Living one's life by the rules. *II, 1*

69. **leisure** Use of time in a way that requires as much skill and concentration as one's work but that totally detaches one from work so that the spontaneous self is free to emerge in a playful and contagious manner. *III, 3*

70. **limitation/acceptance** Giving positive mental assent to the reality that one has boundaries and inabilities. This includes an objective self-awareness of one's strengths and potential as well as weakness and inability. The capacity for self-criticism. *III, 2*

71. **limitation/celebration** The recognition that one's limits are the framework for exercising one's talents. The ability to laugh at one's own imperfections. *III, 3*

72. **loyalty/fidelity** Strict observance of promises and duties to those in authority and to those in close personal relationships. *II, 2*

73. **macroeconomics** The willingness to manage and direct the use of financial resources at an institutional and inter-institutional level toward creating a more stable and equitable world economic order. *IV, 4*

74. **management** The control and manipulation of one's affairs in accordance with one's philosophy and beliefs. It is also the process of giving direction to one's family, institution or business for the purpose of optimizing the institution's goals. *II, 1*

75. **membership/institution** The pride of belonging to and functioning as an integral part of an organization, foundation, establishment, etc. *II, 1*

76. **minessence** The capacity to miniaturize and simplify complex ideas or technological instruments (tools) into concrete and practical objectifications in a way that creatively alters the consciousness of the user. *III, 4*

77. **mission/objectives** The ability to establish organizational goals and execute long term planning that takes into consideration the needs of society and how the organization contributes to those needs. *III, 4*

78. **mutual accountability** The skills to maintain a reciprocal balance of tasks and assignments with others so that everyone is answerable for his/her own area of responsibility. This requires the ability to mobilize one's anger in creative and supportive ways so as to move relationships to increasing levels of cooperation. *III, 4*

79. **mutual/obedience** Being mutually and equally responsible for establishing and being subject to a common set of rules and guidelines in a group of persons. *III, 4*

80. **obedience/duty** Dutifully and submissively complying with moral and legal obligations established by parents and civic and religious authorities. *II, 2*

81. **ownership** Personal and legal possession of skills, decisions, and property that gives one a sense of personal authority. *II, 1*

82. **patriotism/esteem** Honor for one's country based on personal devotion, love and support. *II, 4*

83. **physical delight** The joy of experiencing all the senses of one's body. *I, 3*

84. **pioneerism/innovation** Introducing and originating creative ideas for positive change in social organizations and systems and providing the framework for actualizing them. *III, 3*

85. **play/recreation** A pastime or diversion from the anxiety of day-to-day living for the purpose of undirected, spontaneous refreshment (which provides for a potential self to be experienced). *II, 3*

86. **presence** The ability to be with another person that comes from inner self-knowledge which is so contagious that another person is able to ponder the depths of who he or she is with awareness and clarity. *III, 2*

87. **prestige/image** Physical appearance which reflects success and achievement, gains the esteem of others and promotes success. *II, 2*

88. **productivity** To feel energized by generating and completing tasks and activities and achieving externally established goals and expectations. *II, 1*

89. **property/control** Accumulating property and exercising personal direction over it for security and for meeting one's basic physical and emotional needs. *I, 1*

90. **prophet/vision** The ability to communicate the truth about global issues in such a lucid manner that the hearer is able to transcend his/her limited personal awareness and gain a new perspective on themselves and the needs of the human family. *IV, 4*

91. **quality/evaluation** Appreciating objective self-appraisal and being open to what others reflect back about oneself or team (group) and the products of one's work, as necessary for self-awareness, personal growth, and the improvement of service to others. *III, 2*

92. **reason** The trained capacity to think logically and reasonably based on a formal body of information. The capacity to exercise reason before emotions. *II, 1*

93. **relaxation** Diversion from physical or mental work which reduces stress and provides a balance of work and play as a means of realizing one's potential. *III, 3*

94. **research** Systematic investigation and contemplation of the nature of truths and principles about people and human experience for the purpose of creating new insights and awareness. *III, 2*

95. **responsibility** To be personally accountable for and in charge of a specific area or course of action in one's organization or group. *II, 3*

96. **rights/respect** The moral principle of esteeming the worth (and property) of another as I expect others to esteem me (and mine). *II, 2*

97. **ritual/communication** Skills and use of liturgy and the arts as a communication medium for raising critical consciousness of such themes as world social conditions and awareness of the transcendent. *III, 3*

98. **rule/accountability** The need to have each person openly explain or justify his/her behavior in relationship to the established codes of conduct, procedures, etc. *II, 1*

99. **safety/survival** Concern about the ability to avoid personal injury, danger of loss and to do what is necessary to protect one's self in adverse circumstances. *I, 1*

100. **search/meaning/hope** A personal exploration arising from an inner longing and curiosity to integrate one's feelings, imagination and objective knowledge in order to discover one's unique place in the world. *III, 3*

101. **security** Finding a safe place or relationship where one experiences protection and is free from cares and anxieties. *I, 2*

102. **self actualization** The inner drive toward experiencing and expressing the totality of one's being through spiritual, psychological, physical and mental exercises which enhance the development of one's maximum potential. *III, 3*

103. **Self assertion** The will to put one's self forward boldly regarding a personal line of thought or action. *III, 2*

104. **self Interest/control** Restraining one's feelings and controlling one's personal interests in order to survive physically in the world. *I, 2*

105. **self preservation** Doing what is necessary to protect oneself from physical harm or destruction in an alien world. *I, 1*

106. **self worth** The knowledge that when those one respects and esteems really know him/her, they will affirm that he/she is worthy of that respect. *II, 2*

107. **sensory pleasure/sexuality** Gratifying one's sensual desires and experiencing one's sexual identity. *I, 3*

108. **service/vocation** To be motivated to use one's unique gifts and skills to contribute to society through one's occupation, business, profession or calling. *III, 4*

109. **sharing/listening/trust** The capacity to actively and accurately hear another's thoughts and feelings and to express one's own thoughts and feelings in a climate of mutual confidence in each other's integrity. *III, 2*

110. **simplicity/play** The capacity for deeply appreciating the world combined with a playful attitude toward organizations and systems that is energizing and positive. The ability to see simplicity in complexity and to be detached from the world as primarily material in nature. It can include the mutual sharing of property within a group. *III, 3*

111. **social affirmation** Personal repsect and validation coming from the support and respect of one's peers which is necessary for one to grow and succeed. *II, 4*

112. **support/peer** To have persons that are one's equals that sustain one in both joyful and difficult times. *II, 2*

113. **synergy** Experiencing the relationships of persons within a group to be so harmonious and energized that the outcome of the group far surpasses its predicted ability based on the total abilities of its individual members. *IV, 3*

114. **technology/science** Systematic knowledge of the physical or natural world and practical applications of the knowledge through man-made devices and tools. *II, 1*

115. **territory/security** Provision for physically defending property, a personal domain or nation state. *I, 1*

116. **tradition** Recognizing the importance of ritualizing family history, religious history and national history in one's life so as to enrich its meaning. *II, 4*

117. **transcendence/solitude** Exercising spiritual discipline and detachment so that one experiences a global and visionary perspective due to one's relationship to the universal order. *IV, 3*

118. **truth/wisdom** Intense pursuit and discovery of ultimate truth above all other activities. This results in intimate knowledge of objective and subjective realities which converge into the capacity to clearly comprehend persons and systems and their interrelationship. *IV, 3*

119. **unity/diversity** Recognizing and acting administratively on the belief that an organization is creatively enhanced by giving equal opportunity to persons from a variety of cultures, ethnic backgrounds and diverse training. *III, 4*

120. **unity/uniformity** Harmony and agreement in an institution that is established to achieve efficiency, order, loyalty and conformity to established norms. *II, 4*

121. **wonder/awe/fate** To be filled with marvel, amazement and fear when faced with the overwhelming grandeur and power of one's physical environment. *I, 3*

122. **wonder/curiosity** A sense of marvel and amazement about the physical world coupled with a desire to learn about it and explore it personally. *I, 3*

123. **word** The ability to communicate universal truths so effectively that the hearer becomes conscious of his/her limitations such that life and hope are renewed in the individual hearer. *IV, 3*

124. **work/labor** To have skills and rights that allow one to produce a minimal living for one's self and one's family. *II, 1*

125. **workmanship/art/craft** Skills requiring manual dexterity that produce artifacts and modifies or beautifies person-made environments. *II, 1*

Bibliography

Allport, Gordon W., *The Nature of Prejudice*. New York, Anchor Books Edition, 1958.

Allen, M. J. and Yen, W. M., *Introduction to Measurement Theory*. Monterey, CA.: Brooks/Cole, 1979.

American Psychological Association (APA), *Standards for Education and Psychological Tests*. Washington, DC: Author, 1974.

Anastasl, A., *Psychological Testing (4th edition)*. New York: Macmillan, 1976.

Asch, Solomon E. and Henle, Mary, eds., *The Selected Papers of Wolfgang Kohler*. New York, Liveright, 1969.

Aschenbrenner, George A., "Consciousness Examen." *Review for Religion*, 1972, 31, 14–21.

Ashley, Benedict M. and O'Rourke Kevin D., *Health Care Ethics: A Theological Analysis*. St. Louis: The Catholic Health Association of the United States, 1982.

Assigloli, R., *Psychosynthesis*. New York: The Viking Press, 1971.

Auel, Jean M., *The Clan of the Cave Bear*. Toronto: Bantam Books, 1980.

Bandler, Richard and Grinder, John, *Frogs into Princes: Neuro Linguistic Programming*. Moab, UT: Real People Press, 1979.

———, *The Structure of Magic: A Book About Language and Therapy*. Palo Alto, CA: Science & Behavior Books, Inc., 1975.

Bardwick, Judith M., *Psychology of Women*. New York: Harper & Row, 1971.

Bateson, Gregory, *Steps to an Ecology of Mind*. New York: Ballantine Books, 1972.

Beck, C. M., Crittenden, B. S., and Sullivan, E. V., *Moral Education*. Toronto: University of Toronto Press, 1971.

Bell, Daniel, *The Coming of Post-Industrial Society: A Study in Social Forecasting.* New York: Basic Books, 1973.

Bellah, Robert N., Richard Madsen, William Sullivan, Ann Swindler, and Steven Tipton. *The Good Society.* New York: Knopf, 1991.

Bentov, Itzhak, *Stalking the Wild Pendulum: On the Mechanics of Consciousness.* New York: E. P. Dutton, 1977.

Berger, Peter L., *The Sacred Canopy: Elements of a Sociological Theory of Religion.* New York: Doubleday, 1967.

Blake, Robert F. and Mouton, Jane S., *Consultation: A comprehensive Approach to Organizational Development.* Reading, MA.: Addison-Wesley Publishing Company, 1983.

Blekinsopp, Joseph. *The Men Who Spoke Out.* London: Dalton, 1969.

Boison, Anton T., *The Exploration of the Inner World: A Study of Mental Disorder and Religious Experience.* Philadelphia: University of Pennsylvania Press, 1936.

Bolen, Jean Shinoda, M. D., *Goddesses in Everywoman: A New Psychology of Women.* San Francisco: Harper and Row, Publishers, 1984.

Bradford, Leland P., *Group Development.* La Jolla, CA: University Associates, 1978.

Bronowski, Jacob, *The Ascent of Man.* Boston, Toronto: Little, Brown and Company, 1973.

————, *The Ascent of Man.* Boston, Toronto: Little, Brown, First American Edition, 1974.

Brown, George, *Professor of Education.* Santa Barbara, CA. Unpublished Manuscript.

Brownlie, Ian, ed., *Basic Documents on Human Rights.* Oxford: Clarendon Press, 1971, 1981.

Brueggemann, Walter A., *In Man we Trust: The Neglected Side of Biblical Faith.* Atlanta: John Knox, 1972.

Buckley, Michael, "Rules for Discernment of Spirits." The Way, 1973, 20.

Bugental, James F. T., *The Search for Existential Identity.* San Francisco: Jossey-Bass Publishers, 1976.

Bullock, Alan, *Hitler: A Study in Tyranny.* New York: Harper & Row, Publishers, 1971.

Burke, James, *Connections.* Boston: Little, Brown and Company, 1978.

Burke, W. Warner and Goodstein, Leonard D., ed., *Trends and Issues in OD: Current Theory and Practice.* San Diego, CA: University Associates, Inc., 1980.

Cada, Lawrence, et al., *Shaping the Coming Age of Religious Life.* New York: The Seabury Press, 1979.

Campbell, D. T., and Fiske, D. W., "Convergent and Discriminant Validation by the Mltitrait-Multimethod Matrix." *Psychological Bulletin,* 1959, 56, 81–105.

Campbell, Joseph, ed., *The Portable Jung*. New York: Penguin Books, 1971.

Cantin, Eileen, Mounier, *A Personalist View of History*. New York, Paulist Press, 1974.

Caplan, G. and Killilea, M., editors, *Support Systems and Mutual Help*. New York: Grune and Stratton, 1972.

Caplan, Ruth B. et al., *Helping the Helpers to Help: Mental Health Consultation to Aid Clergymen in Pastoral Work*. New York: The Seabury Press, 1972.

Capra, Fritjof, *The Turning Point*. New York: Bantam Books, 1982.

Carretto, Carol, *Letters from the Desert*. Maryknoll, New York: Orbis Books, 1972.

Carroll, Lewis, *Alice's Adventures in Wonderland*. London, Macmillan, 1963.

Casslrer, Ernst, *The Philosophy of Symbolic Forms*. New Haven and London: Yale University Press, 1957.

Chodorow, Nancy, "Family Structure and Feminine Personality." In M. Z. Rosaldo and L. Lamphere, eds., *Woman, Culture and Society*. Stanford: Stanford University Press, 1974.

———, *The Reproduction of Mothering*. University of California Press, 1978.

Cleremont de Castillejo, Irene, *Knowing Woman*. New York: Harper & Row, 1973.

Clark, Kenneth, *Civilization*. New York and Evanston. Harper & Row, Publishers, 1969.

———, *Civilization: A Personal View*. New York, Harper and Row, 1972.

Clements, R. E., *Prophecy and Covenant*. Naperville, IL.: Allenson, 1965.

Clinebell, Howard, *Contemporary Growth Therapies*. Nashville: Abingdon, 1981.

Corey, Gerald, Corey, Marianne S., and Callanan, Pabick, *Issues and Ethics in the Helping Professions*. Monterey, CA: Brooks/Cole Publishing Company, 1984.

Covey, Stephen R., *The Seven Habits of Highly Effective People*. New York: Simon and Schuster, 1990.

Cox, Sue, *Female Psychology: The Emerging Self*. Chicago: Science Research Associates, 1976.

Crenshaw, James L., ed., *Studies in Ancient Israelite Wisdom*. New York: Klav, 1976.

Cronbach, L. J., "Coefficient Alpha and the Internal Structure of Tests." *Psychometrika*, 1951, 16, 297–334.

———, "Validity on Parole: How Can We Go Straight?" *New Directions for Testing and Measurement*, 1980, 5, 99–108.

———, *Essentials of Psychological Testing (3rd Edition)*. New York: Harper & Row, 1970.

Cronbach, L. J., and Meehl, P. E., "Construct Validity in Psychological Tests." *Psychological Bulletin*, 1955, 52, 281–302.

Crystal, John C. and Bolles, Richard N., *Where Do I Go From Here With My Life?* Berkeley: Ten Speed Press, 1974.

Davies, Paul, *God and the New Physics.* New York: Simon & Schuster, Inc., 1983.

de Chardin, Pierre Teilhard, *Le Milieu Divin: An Essay on the Interior Life.* New York: Harper & Brothers, 1960.

de Guibert, *Theology of the Spiritual Life.* New York: Sheed and Ward, 1954.

de Laszlo, Violet S., ed., *Psyche and Symbol: A Selection from the Writings of C. G. Jung.* Garden City, New York: Doubleday, 1958.

de Saint-Exupery, Antoine, *The Wisdom of the Sands.* New York: Harcourt, Brace and Company, 1950.

Deal, Terrence E. and Kennedy, Allan A., *Corporate Cultures: The Rites and Rituals of Corporate Life.* Reading, MA.: Addison-Wesley Publishing Company, 1982.

Dinnerstein, Dorothy, *The Mermaid and the Minotaur: Sexual Arrangements and Human Malaise.* New York: Harper & Row, 1977.

Dix, Dorn Gregory, *The Shape of the Liturgy.* London: Dacre Press, 1945.

Douglas, Ann, *The Feminization of American Culture.* New York: Avon Books, 1977.

Dunnette, M. D., and Borman, W. C. "Personnel Selection and Classification Systems." *Annual Review of Psychology,* 1979, 30, 477, 525.

Dyer, William G., *Contemporary Issues in Management and Organization Development.* Reading, Mass.: Addison-Wesley Publishing Company, 1983.

Edward, Joyce, Ruskin, Turrinl, *Separation-Individuation: Theory and Application.* New York: Gardner Press, 1981.

Elgin, Duane, *Voluntary Simplicity: An Ecological Lifestyle that Promotes Personal and Social Renewal.* Toronto and New York: Bantam Books, 1982.

Erikson, Erik H., ed., *Adulthood.* New York: W. W. Norton & Company, Inc. 1978.

———, *Childhood and Society.* New York: W. W. Norton & Company, Inc., 1950, 1963.

———, *Gandhi's Truth.* New York: W. W. Norton & Company, Inc., 1969.

———, *Identity: Youth and Crises.* New York: W. W. Norton & Company, Inc., 1968.

———, *Identity and the Life Cycle.* New York: W. W. Norton & Company, Inc., 1980.

Fabry, Joseph B., *The Pursuit of Meaning: Logotherapy Applied to Life.* Boston: Beacon Press, 1968.

The First International Conference on Moral and Religious Development, *Toward Moral and Religious Maturity.* Morristown, NJ: Silver Burdett Company, 1980.

Fleming, David L., *A Contemporary Reading of the Spiritual Exercises*. St. Louis: The Institute of Jesuit Sources, 1976.

Ford, George A. and Lippitt, Gordon, *Planning Your Future*. La Jolla: University Associates, 1972.

Fowler, James W., *Stages of Faith*, San Francisco: Harper & Row, Publishers, 1981.

Frankl, Viktor E., *The Doctors and the Soul*. New York: Vintage Books, 1955, 1965.

————, *Man's Search for Meaning*. New York: Simon & Schuster, 1959.

————, *Man's Search for Meaning*. Boston, Beacon Press, 1963.

————, *Psychotherapy and Existentialism*. New York: Simon & Schuster, 1967.

Freire, Paulo, *Education for Critical Consciousness*. Translated by Myra Ramos. *The Pedagogy of the Oppressed*. Translated by Myra Ramos. New York, Seabury Press, 1971.

————, *Pedagogy in Process*. New York: Seabury Press, 1978.

————, *Pedagogy of the Oppressed*. New York: Herder and Herder, 1972.

French, Wendell L. and Bell, Cecil H., Jr., *Organization Development*. Englewood Cliffs: Prentice-Hall, Inc., 1978.

Friars Minor of the Franciscan Province of Saint Barbara, translators. *Early Franciscan Classics*. Peterson, New Jersey: Saint Anthony Guild Press, 1962.

Friday, Nancy, *My Mother/My Self*. New York: Dell Books, 1978.

Friedman, H. S. "On Shutting One's Eyes to Face Validity." *Psychological Bulletin*, 1983, 94, 185–187.

Fromm, Erich, *The Anatomy of Human Destructiveness*. New York: Holt, Rinehart and Winston, 1973.

————, *Escape From Freedom*. New York and Toronto, Rinehart and Company, Inc., 1941.

————, *The Heart of Man*. New York: Perennial Library, 1964.

Frondizi, Risieri, *What is Value? An Introduction to Axiology*. Translated by Solomon Lipp. LaSalle, IL, Open Court, 1971.

Gardner, Howard, *Frames of Mind: The Theory of Multiple Intelligences*. New York: Harper Basic Books, 1985.

————, *The Unschooled Mind: How Children Think and How Schools Should Teach*. New York: Harper Basic Books, 1991.

————, *Spiritual Connections*. Dayton, OH: Values Technology, 1991.

Gelatt, H. B., Barbara Varenhorst, Richard Carey, and Gordon P. Miller, *Decisions and Outcomes*. Princeton: College Entrance Examination Board, 1973.

Gerbault, Alain, *Firecrest: Round the World*. New York: David McKay Company, Inc., 1981.

Gerstein, Martin, Pappen-Daniel, *Understanding Adulthood*. Fullerton, CA: California Personnel and Guidance Association, 1981.

Ghiselli, E. E., *Theory of Psychological Measurement*. New York: McGraw-Hill, 1964.

Gilligan, Carol, *In a Different Voice*. Cambridge, Massachusetts: Harvard University Press, 1982.

Glasser, William, *Reality Therapy: A New Approach to Psychiatry*. New York: Harper and Row, 1965.

———, *Control Theory in the Classroom*. New York: Harper & Row, 1986.

Gordon, Thomas, *P.E.T.: Parent Effectiveness Training*. New York: New American Library, 1975.

Gould, Roger L., *Transformations: Growth and Change in Adult Life*. New York: Simon & Schuster, 1978.

Goulet, Denis, "An Ethical Model For The Study of Values," *Harvard Educational Review*, Vol. 41, no. 2, 1971.

Green, Thomas H., S. J., *Weeds Among the Wheat Discernment: Where Prayer and Action Meet*. Notre Dame: Ave Maria Press, 1984.

Hall, Brian P., *Developing Leadership by Stages: A Value-Based Approach to Executive Management*. London and New Delhi: Manohar Publications, 1979.

———, *The Development of Consciousness: A Confluent Theory of Values*. New York: Paulist Press, 1976.

———, *The Genesis Effect: Personal and Organizational Transformations*. Mahwah, NJ: Paulist Press, 1986.

———, *Shepherds and Lovers*. Ramsey, NJ: Paulist Press, 1982.

———, *The Personal Discernment Inventory*. New York: Paulist Press, 1980.

———, *The Wizard of Maldoone*. New York: Paulist Press, 1976.

———, *Value Clarification as Learning Process: A Sourcebook*. New York: Paulist Press, 1973.

Hall, Brian P. and Tonna, Benjamin, *God's Plans for Us: A Practical Strategy for Discernment of Spirits*. New York: Paulist Press, 1980.

Hall, Brian P. and Thompson, Helen, *Leadership through Values: An Approach to Personal and Organizational Development*. New York: Paulist Press, 1980.

Hall, Brian P. and Osburn, Joseph, *Nog's Vision*. New York: Paulist Press, 1976.

Hall, Brian P. and Smith, Maury, *Value Clarification as Learning Process: Handbook for Clergy and Christian Educators*. New York: Paulist Press, 1973.

Harari, Oren., "A Hybrid Left-Brain/Right-Brain Approach to Validity." *The Genesis Effect*, pp. 275–286.

Haught, John F., *The Cosmic-Adventure.* New York/Ramsey: Paulist Press, 1984.

Haughton, Rosemary, *On Trying to Be Human.* 1966. Springfield, IL, Templegate, 1966.

Havighurst, Robert J., *Development Tasks and Education. Third Edition.* New York, David McKay, 1972.

Hayes, William L., *Quantification in Psychology.* Belmont, CA, Wordsworth Publishing, 1967.

Heschel, A., *The Prophets.* New York: Harper & Row, 1963.

Hillman, James, *The Dream and the Underworld.* New York: Harper & Row, Publishers, 1979.

Hollard, James G., "A Quantitative Measure for Programmed Instruction." *American Educational Research Journal*, 1967, Vol. 4, pp. 87–101.

Howe, Ruel L., *Man's Need and God's Action.* Greenwich, CT: The Seabury Press, 1953.

Hutchins, Robert Maynard, ed., *Great Books of the Western World.* Chicago: Encyclopedia Britannica, 1952.

Ignatlous of Loyola, *The Spiritual Exercises of St. Ignatius.* Louis J. Publ (tr.). Westminster, Maryland: Newman Press, (no. 169).

Illich, Ivan, *Celebration of Awareness.* New York: Doubleday & Company, 1969.

———, *Deschooling Society.* New York: Harper & Row, Publishers, 1971.

———, *Gender.* New York: Pantheon Books, 1982.

———, *Interpersonal Relational Networks.* C.I.D.O.C., No. 1014, Tools For Conviviality. New York, Harper and Row, 1973.

———, *Tools for Conviviality.* New York: Harper & Row, Publishers, 1973.

———, *Toward a History of Needs.* New York: Pantheon Books, 1978.

Isgar, Tom and Susan, *Learning Games.* Washington, DC: United States National Student Association, to date.

Jackson, Paul, S. J., ed., *Sharafuddin Maneri: The Hundred Letters.* New York: Paulist Press, 1980.

Jaynes, Julian, *The Origin of Consciousness in the Breakdown of the Bicameral Mind.* Boston: Houghton Mifflin Company, 1976.

Johnson, David W., Johnson, Roger T. and Johnson Holubec, Edythe, *Circles of Learning: Cooperation in the Classroom.* Interaction Book Company, 1986.

———, *Teaching Students to be Peacemakers.* Interaction Book Company, 1991.

Johnston, William, *Silent Music: The Science of Mediation.* New York: Harper & Row, Publishers, 1974.

Jung, Carl G., *Collected Works.* Bollingen Series, New York: Pantheon Books, 153–354.

———, *Memories, Dreams, Reflections.* New York: Pantheon Books, 1963.

———, *Psychological Types; or, The Psychology of Individuation.* Trans. H. Godwin Baynes, New York: Harcourt, Brace and Company, Inc., 1923.

———, *Tipi Psicologici.* Universale Scientifica (translated by Cesare L. Musalti and Lulgi Aurigemma). Editor Boringhieri, Torino, 1977.

Kaiser, Hellmuth, ed. by Flerman, Louis B., *Effective Psychotherapy.* New York: The Free Press, 1965.

Kaplan, R. M. and Saccuzzo, D. P., *Psychological Testing: Principles, Applications, and Issues.* Monterey, CA: Brooks/Cole, 1982.

Keirsey, D. and Bates, M., *Please Understand Me: An Essay on Temperament Styles.* Del Mar: Prometheus Nemesis Books, 1978.

Kelsey, Morton T., *Gods, Dreams, and Revelation: A Christian Interpretation of Dreams.* First edition published in 1968 under the title: *Dreams: The Dark Speech of the Spirit.* Minneapolis: Augsburg Publishing House, 1973, 1974.

Kerlinger, F. N., *Behavioral Research: A Conceptual Approach.* New York: Holt, Rinehart, & Winston, 1978.

Kimper, Frank, Professor of Pastoral Counseling, Claremont, CA, Private Paper, 1969.

Kirschenbaum, Howard, *Advanced Value Clarification.* La Jolla, CA: University Associates, 1977.

———, *On Becoming Carl Rogers.* New York: Delacorte Press, 1979.

Knapp, Clifford, "Attitudes and Values in Environmental Education." *The Journal of Environmental Education.* Vol. 3, 1972, pp. 26–29.

Koch, Kenneth, *I Never Told Anybody. Teaching Poetry in a Nursing Home.* New York: Random House, 1977.

———, *Rose, Where Did You Get That Red? Teaching Great Poetry to Children.* New York: Random House, 1973.

———, *Wishes, Lies and Dreams: Teaching Children to Write Poetry.* New York: Vintage Books, 1970.

Koestenbaum, Peter, *Existential Sexuality: Choosing to Love.* Englewood Cliffs: Prentice-Hall, 1974.

———, *The New Image of the Person,* Westport, CT: Greenwood Press, 1978.

Kohlberg, Lawrence, In C. M. Beck, B. S. Crittenden and E. V. Sullivan (eds.), *Moral Education*. Toronto: University of Toronto Press, 1971.

————, *The Concepts of Developmental Psychology As A Central Guide To Education: Examples From Cognitive and Psychological Education*. Institute for Human Development, Harvard University.

————, *The Philosophy of Moral Development*. San Francisco: Harper and Row, 1981.

Kraeling, Emil, *The Prophets*. Chicago: Rand McNally, 1969.

Langer, Susanne K., *Philosophy in a New Key*. Cambridge: Harvard University Press, 1957.

Leech, Kenneth, *Soul Friend*. San Francisco: Harper & Row, 1977.

Lee, Dorothy, *Valuing the Self*. Englewood Cliffs, New Jersey: Prentice-Hall, Inc., 1976.

LeShan, Lawrence, *How to Mediate: A Guide to Self-Discovery*. New York: Bantam Books, 1975.

Leslie, Robert E., *Jesus and Logotherapy*. New York, Nashville: Abingdon Press, 1965.

Lever, Janet, "Sex Differences in the Complexity of Children's Play and Games." *American Sociological Review*, 1978, 43, pp. 471–483.

————, "Sex Differences in the Games Children Play." *Social Problems*, 1976, 223, pp. 418–487.

Levinson, Daniel, *The Seasons of a Man's Life*. New York: Alfred A. Knopf, 1978.

Lewis, Howard R. and Harold S. Streitfeld, *Growth Games: How To Tune In Yourself, Your Family, Your Friends*. New York: Bantam Books, 1972.

Lewis, Hunter, *A Question of Values*. New York: Harper & Row, 1990.

Likona, Thomas, ed., *Moral Development and Behavior: Theory, Research, and Social Issues*. New York: Holt, Rinehart and Winston, 1976.

Lindblom, Johannes, *Prophecy in Ancient Israel*. Philadelphia: Fortress, 1965.

Lippitt, Gordon L., *Visualizing Change: Model Building and the Change Process*. Fairfax, VA, NTL Learning Resource Co., 1973.

Lowen, Alexander, *Narcissism: Denial of the True Self*. New York: Macmillan Publishing Company, 1983.

Loye, David, *The Sphinx and the Rainbow: Brain, Mind and Future Vision*. Boulder, CO: Shambhala Publications, Inc., 1983.

Luthe, Wolfgang, and Schultz, Johannes, *Autogenic Therapy*. Vol. 1. New York, Grune and Stratton, 1970.

Lyons, Gracie, *Constructive Criticism*. Berkeley: Issues in Radical Therapy, 1976.

Maccoby, Eleanor, ed., *The Development of Sex Differences*. Stanford: Stanford University Press, 1966.

Mahler, Margaret, *Essays in Honor of Margaret S. Mahler: Separation-Individuation*. New York: International University Press, 1971.

——, *On Human Symbiosis: The Vicissitudes of Individuation*. New York: Lane Medical Library, 1968.

——, *The Psychological Birth of the Human Infant*. New York. Basic Books, 1975.

Malatesta, Edward, ed., *Discernment of Spirits*. Collegeville, MN: Liturgical Press, 1970.

Maly, Eugene, *Prophets of Salvation*. New York: Herder, 1969.

Margolis, Maxine, *Mothers and Such: Views of American Women and Why They Changed*. Berkeley: University of California Press, 1984.

Maslow, Abraham, ed. by Richard J. Lowry, *Dominance, Self-esteem, Self-actualization: Germinal Papers of A. H. Maslow*. Monterey, CA: Brooks/ Cole Publishing Company, 1973.

——, *The Farther Reaches of Human Nature*. New York: Viking Press, 1971.

——, *Motivation and Personality*. New York: Harper and Row, 1954, 1970.

——, ed., *New Knowledge in Human Values*. New York: Penguin Books, 1959.

——, *Religions, Values, and Peak-Experiences*. New York: Penguin Books, 1964, 1976.

——, *Toward a Psychology of Being*. Jersey City, NJ: Van Nostrand, 1962.

——, *Toward a Psychology of Being*. New York: Van Norstand, 1968.

——, *Toward A Psychology of Being*. Second Edition. Cincinnati, OH, Van Nostrand Reinhold, 1968.

May, Herbert G., and Metzger, Bruce M., eds., *The New Oxford Annotated Bible With The Apocrypha*. New York: Oxford University Press, 1962.

May, Rollo, *The Meaning of Anxiety*. New York: Washington Square Press. Pocket Books, 1950, 1977.

McGregor, Douglas, *The Human Side of Enterprise*. New York: McGraw-Hill, 1960.

Messick, S., "Test Validity and the Ethics of Assessment." *American Psychologist*, 180, 35, 1012–1027.

Miller, Sherod, Elam W. Nunnally, and Daniel B. Wackman, *Alive and Aware: How To Improve Your Relationships Through Better Communication*. Minneapolis: Interpersonal Communication Programs, Inc., 1975.

Myers, I. B., *Gifts Differing*. Palo Alto: Consulting Psychologists Press, Inc., 1980.

Miller, Jean Baker, *Toward a New Psychology of Women*, Boston: Beacon Press, 1976.

Milne, A. A., *The House at Pooh Corner*. Revised Edition. New York, E. P. Dutton, 1961.

Minuchin, Salvador, et al., *Families of the Slums: An Exploration of Their Structure Treatment*. New York, Basic Books, 1967.

Mische, Gerald and Mische, Patricia, *Toward a Human World Order*. New York: Paulist Press, 1977.

Mounler, Emmanuel, *The Character of Man*. Translated by Cynthia Rowland. New York, Harper Bros., 1956.

Moustakas, Clark E., *The Self Explorations in Personal Growth*. New York, Harper and Row, 1956.

Mowvley, Harry, *Reading the Old Testament Prophets Today*. Atlanta: John Knox, 1979.

Mumford, Lewis, *The City In History*. New York, Harcourt, Brace and World, 1961.

Murphy, J. M. and Gilligan, C., "Moral Development in Late Adolescence and Adulthood: A Critique and Reconstruction of Kohlberg's Theory." *Human Development*, 1980, 23, pp. 77–104.

Murphy, Roland, *Seven Books of Wisdom*. Milwaukee: Bruce, 1960.

Naisbitt, John, *Megatrends*. New York: Warner Books, 1982.

Needleham, Jacob, translator, *Being-in-the-World: Selected Papers of Ludwig Binswanger*. New York: Harper Torchbooks.

Neumann, Erich, *The Origins and History of Consciousness*. R. F. C. Hull, trans. Princeton: Princeton University Press, 1954.

Nicholls, J., Pearl, R. A., and Licht, B. G., "On the Validity of Inferences About Personality Constructs." *Psychological Bulletin*, 1983, 94, 188–190.

Oden, Thomas C., *The Structures of Awareness*. Nashville, Abingdon Press, 1969.

———, *Game Free: A Guide to the Meaning of Intimacy*. New York, Harper and Row, 1974.

O'Leary, Virginia E., *Toward Understanding Women*. Monterey, CA, Brooks/Cole, 1977.

Ouchi, William G., *Theory 2: How American Business Can Meet the Japanese Challenge*. Reading, MA: Addison-Wesley Publishing Company, 1981.

———, *The M-Form Society: How American Teamwork Can Capture the Competitive Edge*. Reading, Massachusetts: Addison-Wesley Publishing Company, 1981.

———, *The M-Form Society: How American Teamwork Can Capture the Competitive Edge*. Reading, Massachusetts: Addison-Wesley Publishing Company, 1984.

Ornstein, R., *The Psychology of Consciousness*. San Francisco: Freeman, 1975.

Panzarella, Andrew, *Microcosm, A Radical Experiment in ReEducation for Becoming a Person.* Winona, MN: St. Mary's College Press, 1972.

Parnes, Sidney J., *Creative Behavior Guidebook.* New York: Scribner's, 1967.

Peck, M. S., *People of the Lie: The Hope for Healing Human Evil.* New York: Simon & Schuster, 1983.

Perls, Fritz S., *Gestalt Therapy Verbatim.* New York: Bantam Books, 1972.

Peters, Thomas J. and Waterman, Robert H. Jr., *In Search of Excellence.* New York: Warner Books, 1982.

Pfeiffer, J. William, and Goodstein, Leonard D., ed., *The 1984 Annual. Developing Human Resources.* San Diego, CA: University Associates, 1984.

Pfeiffer, J. William and John E. Jones, *A Handbook of Structured Experiences for Human Relations Training.* Vol. 1. La Jolla: University Associates, 1969.

————, *The 1980 Annual Handbook for Group Facilitators.* San Diego: University Associates, 1980. See also *Annuals* for 1972–1979; 1981.

Phenix, Philip, *Man and His Becoming.* University of Puget Sound, Tacoma, Wa., The Brown and Haley Lectures, Twelfth Series. New Brunswick, NJ, Rutgers University Press, 1964.

Piaget, J., *The Language and Thought of the Child* (translated by M. Gabain). New York: Harcourt Brace, 1932.

Poulain, Augustin F., *The Graces of Interior Prayer.* Trans. Leonora L. Yorke Smith. Westminster, Ve.: Celtic Cross Books, 1978.

Pressey, Sidney, "Development and Appraisal of Devices Providing Immediate Automatic Scoring of Objective Tests and Concomitant Self Instruction." *Journal of Psychology,* April 1950.

Previte-Orton, C. W., *The Shorter Cambridge Medieval History. Volumes I & II.* Great Britain: Cambridge University Press, 1953.

Progoff, Ira, *The Symbolic and the Real: A New Psychological Approach to the Fuller Experience of Personal Existence.* New York: McGraw-Hill, 1963, 1973.

————, *The Practice of Process Meditation: The Intensive Journal Way to Spiritual Experience.* New York: Dialogue House Library, 1980.

Rad, Gerhard von, *The Message of the Prophets.* New York: Harpers, 1977, 1965.

————, *Wisdom in Israel.* James Martin, trans. Nashville: Abingdon, 1972.

Rahner, Hugo. *Ignatius the Theologian.* London: Chapman, 1968.

Raths, Louis E., Harmin, Merrill, and Simon, Sidney B., *Values and Teaching: Working with Values in the Classroom.* Columbus, OH: Charles E. Merrill Publishing Company, 1966.

Rawls, John, *A Theory of Justice.* Cambridge: Harvard University Press, 1971.

Reeves, Clement, *The Psychology of Rollo May.* San Francisco: Jossey-Bass Publishers, 1977.

Reid, David P., *What Are They Saying About the Prophets?* New York: Paulist Press, 1980.

Rescher, Nicholas, *Introduction to Value Theory.* Englewood Cliffs, NJ: Prentice-Hall, 1969.

Restak, R., "The Hemispheres of the Brain Have Minds of Their Own." *New York Times,* January 25, 1976.

Richards, Sister Innocentia, Ph.D., *Discernment of Spirits,* Collegeville, Minnesota: The Liturgical Press, 1970.

Roberts, David E., *Psychotherapy and a Christian View of Man.* New York: Charles Scribner's Sons, 1950.

Rogers, Carl, *On Becoming A Person.* Boston, Houghton Mifflin, 1970.

Rokeach, Milton, *Beliefs, Attitudes and Values: A Theory of Organization and Change.* San Francisco: Jossey-Bass, 1968.

———, *The Nature of Human Values.* New York: Free Press, 1973.

———, *The Three Christs of Ypsilanti: A Psychological Study.* New York: Knopf, 1964.

———, Bonier, Richard, et al., *The Open and Closed Mind: Investigations into the Nature of Belief Systems and Personality Systems.* New York: Basic Books, 1960.

Rokeach, Milton, ed., *Understanding Human Values: Individual and Societal.* New York: Free Press, 1979.

Rosen, L., Hall, Brian, Kalven, J., Taylor, B., *Readings in Value Development.* New York/ Ramsey: Paulist Press, 1982.

———, *Value Development—A Practical Guide.* New York/Ramsey: Paulist Press, 1982.

Ross, Maggle, *The Fire of Your Life.* New York: Paulist Press, 1983.

Rubin, Lillian, *Intimate Strangers: Men and Women Together.* New York: Harper & Row, 1983.

———, *Worlds of Pain.* New York: Basic Books, 1976.

Ruch, Richard S. and Goodman, Ronald, *Image at the Top.* New York: The Free Press, 1983.

Ryckman, Richard M., *Theories of Personality.* New York: D. Van Nostrand Company, 1978.

Sakaiya, Taichi, *The Knowledge Value Revolution, or, a History of the Future.* Tokyo: Kodansha International, 1991.

Satir, Virginia, *Making Contact.* Millbrae, CA: Celestial Arts, 1976.

———, *Peoplemaking.* Palo Alto: Science and Behavior Books, 1972.

Sarte, Jean-Paul, *Being and Nothingness: An Essay on Phenomenological Ontology*. New York: Washington Square Press, 1953, 1956.

Sax, Seville and Sandra Hollander, *Reality Games: Games People Ought to Play*. New York: Popular Library, 1972.

Scarf, Maggie, *Unfinished Business*. New York: Doubleday and Co., Inc., 1980.

Schein, Edgar R., *Organizational Culture and Leadership*. San Francisco: Jossey-Bass, 1992.

Schiller, Friedrich, *Naive and Sentimental Poetry and On the Sublime*. Translated and edited by Julius A. Elias. New York, Ungar, 1966.

Schlegel, Richard, "Quantum Physics and Human Purpose." *Zygon*, Volume 8, nos. 3 and 4, September–December, 1973.

Schumacher, E. F., *A Guide for the Perplexed*. New York: Harper & Row, 1977.

———, *Small is Beautiful*. New York: Harper & Row, 1973.

Scott, R. B. Y., *The Relevance of the Prophets*. New York: Macmillan, 1968.

———, *The Way of Wisdom in the Old Testament*. New York: Macmillan, 1971.

Sebald, Hans, *Momism: The Silent Disease of America*. Chicago: Nelson Hall Co., 1976.

Sheehy, Gail, *Passages*. New York: Dutton, 1976.

Simon, Sidney B., Howe, Leland W., and Kirschenbaum, Howard, *Values Clarification: A Handbook of Practical Strategies of Teachers and Students*. New York: Hart Publishing Company, 1972.

Skinner, B. F., *Verbal Behavior*. New York: Appleton-Century-Crofts, 1957.

Sobel, Robert, *I.B.M. Colossus in Transition*. New York: Bantam Books, 1983.

Society of Saint Francis. *Manual of the Third Order of Saint Francis*. England: The Society of Saint Francis.

Soleri, Paolo, *Arcology: The City in the Image of Man*. Cambridge MA: MIT Press, 1969.

———, *The Arcology of Paolo Soleri*. Cambridge, MA: The MIT Press, 1972.

Sowa, J. F., *Conceptual Structures: Information Processing in Mind and Machine*. Palo Alto, CA: Addison-Wesley Publishing Company, 1984.

Spence, J. T., and Helmreich, R. I., "Beyond Face Validity: A Solution." *Psychological Bulletin*. 1983, 94, 181–184.

Spencer, Anita, *Mothers Are People Too: A Contemporary Analysis of Motherhood*. New York: Paulist Press, 1984.

———, *Seasons: Women's Search for Self through Life's Stages*. New York: Paulist Press, 1984.

Sperry, R. W., "Science and the Problem of Values," *Zygon*, Volume 9, no. 1, March, 1974.

Springer, S., *Left Brain, Right Brain*. San Francisco: Freeman, 1981.

Stack, Carol B., *All Our Kin*. New York: Harper & Row, 1974.

Stevens, Edward, *Business Ethics*. New York: Paulist Press, 1979.

Stevens, John O., *Awareness, Exploring, Experimenting, Experiencing*. Moab, UT: Real People Press, 1972.

Tenopyr, M. L., "Content-construct Confusion." *Personnel Psychology* 1977, 30, 47–54.

Terkel, Studs, *Working*. New York, Pantheon Books, 1972.

Thera, Nyanaponika, *The Heart of Buddhist Meditation*. New York, Samuel Weiser, 1970.

Tillich, Paul, *The Courage To Be*. New Haven and London: Yale University Press, 1952.

Toffler, Alvin, *Future Shock*. New York: Random House, 1970.

———, *Power Shift*. New York: Bantam Books, 1990.

Tondow, Murray and Orten, Marilyn, *Social Process Framework*. Chicago: Follet Press, 1960.

Toner, Jules, S. J., *A Commentary on St. Ignatius' Rules for the Discernment of Spirits*. St. Louis: The Institute of Jesuit Sources, 1982.

Tonna, Benjamin, *Gospel for the Cities: A Socio-Theology of Urban Ministry*. Translated by William E. Jerman, Ata. Maryknoll, New York: Orbis Books, 1982.

Torrance, E. Paul, *Torrance Tests of Creative Thinking*. Princeton: Personal Press, Inc., 1966.

Tournier, Paul, *The Meaning of Persons*. New York: Harper & Row, 1957.

Townsend, Robert, "Don't Just Do Something." *Center Magazine*, Volume 2, 1970.

Underhill, Evelyn, *Misticism*. New York: Meridian Books, 1955. "Uniform Guidelines on Employee Selection Procedures." Federal Register, 1978, 43, 38296–38309.

Vaillant, George, *Adaptation to Life*. Boston: Little, Brown and Co., 1977.

Van der Hoop, J. H., *Conscious Orientation*. New York: Harcourt Brace, 1939.

Vargas, Julie S., "Instructional Design Flaws in Computer Assisted Instruction." *Phi Delta Kappan*, 1986. Vol. 67, pp. 738–744.

Vargas, Julie S., "Stimulus Control in Instructional Design." W. Heward, et al., editors. *Focus on Behavior Analysis in Education*. Westerville, OH: Charles Merrill, 1984.

Vaughn, F., *Awakening Intuition*. New York: Anchor Books. Doubleday, 1979.

Wadsworth, Barry J., *Piaget's Theory of Cognitive Development*. New York: David McKay Company, Inc., 1971.

Wagner, Richard, *Environment and Man*. New York, W. W. Norton, 1971.

Wheatly, Margaret J., *Leadership and the New Science*. San Francisco: Berrett-Koehler, 1992.

Weber, Max, *The Protestant Ethic and the Spirit of Capitalism*. Talcott Parsons, trans. London: George Allen & Unwin, 1976.

Wheeler, Daniel D., and Janis, Irving, L., *A Practical Guide for Making Decisions*. New York: Free Press, 1980.

Wheeler, Harvey, *Center Report*, 1974. Center for Democratic Institutions, Santa Barbara, CA.

Wigginton, Eliot, ed. *The Foxfire Book*. New York, Anchor Books Edition, 1972.

Wilber, Ken, *A Sociable God*. New York: New Press, 1983.

Wilson, Robert R., *Prophecy and Society in Ancient Israel*. Philadelphia: Fortress, 1980.

Wright, John H., "Discernment of Spirits in the New Testament." *Communio*, 1974, 1, #2.

Wolf, Fred Alan, *Star Wayne: Mind, Consciousness, and Quantum Physics*. New York: Macmillan Publishing Company, 1984.

Wyssm, Dieter, *Depth Psychology: A Critical History*. New York: W. W. Norton and Company, Inc., 1966.

Yalom, Irvin D., *Existential Psychotherapy*. New York: Basic Books, Inc., 1980.

———, *Inpatient Group Psychotherapy*. New York: Basic Books, 1983.

———, *The Theory and Practice Group Psychotherapy*. New York: Basic Books, 1975.